WHEN MY BROTHERS COME HOME

WESLEYAN POETRY

WHEN
MY BROTHERS
COME HOME

POEMS FROM CENTRAL AND
SOUTHERN AFRICA

EDITED BY

FRANK MKALAWILE CHIPASULA

 WESLEYAN UNIVERSITY PRESS

Middletown, Connecticut

Copyright © 1985 by Frank Chipasula

All rights reserved.

Illustration based on a detail of mosaic mural, *Seikoeivei* by Sash

Information on source and copyright can be found at the end of each
poem.

Library of Congress Cataloging in Publication Data
Main entry under title:

When my brothers come home.

1. African poetry (English)—Africa, Central.
2. African poetry (English)—Africa, Southern.
3. African poetry (Portuguese)—Translations into
English. 4. English poetry—Translations from
Portuguese. 5. Africa—Poetry. I. Chipasula, Frank.
PR9346.W48   1985   820'.8'0896   83–21832
ISBN 0–8195–5092–2 (alk. paper)
ISBN 0–8195–6089–8 (pbk. : alk. paper)

All inquiries and permission requests should be addressed to the Publisher,
Wesleyan University Press, 110 Mt. Vernon Street,
Middletown, Connecticut 06457.

Distributed by Harper & Row Publishers, Keystone Industrial Park,
Scranton, Pennsylvania 18512.

Manufactured in the United States of America

FIRST EDITION
Wesleyan Poetry
First Wesleyan Paperback

For Pat
> my wife and compatriot

and Masauko
> my son, my mirror

To the memory of
> Josina Machel
> Agostinho Neto
> Eduardo Mondlane

"Our dream is the size of freedom."

CONTENTS

ix

PREFACE

NO LITERARY INVESTMENT of the magnitude of this anthology can be made without the investor simultaneously incurring both visible and invisible debts. All literary work should, ideally, be performed collectively. The following are some of the people who collaborated in the realization of this book. Jeannette Hopkins, my publisher at Wesleyan University Press, not only showed a keen personal interest in the poetry, but also, through her firmness and probing questions, helped me reach greater clarity in achieving my goals. Professors Michael S. Harper and Lawrence F. Sykes, master image-makers, of Brown University and Rhode Island College respectively, recognized my capacity for shouldering responsibilities and encouraged me in many tangible ways, too numerous to itemize here. Professor Harper, as my teacher in the Graduate Writing Program at Brown, accepted the anthology as a viable Independent Study Project and allowed me time to do further research for it. More encouragement and support came from Ms. Toni Morrison, of Random House, in New York, Ms. Nadine Gordimer, and Dr. Es'kia Mphahlele.

This book belongs to all the poets, dead and alive, and to the old continent. Whatever errors of judgment there may be in the book are mine, and I am solely responsible for them. I am the victim who was chosen to shoulder the burden and I did not falter.

FRANK MKALAWILE CHIPASULA
Providence, Rhode Island
April 1983

WHEN
MY BROTHERS
COME HOME

INTRODUCTION

THIS VOLUME attempts to contextualize and harmonize the most significant and representative poetic voices of Central and Southern Africa by creating a common regional forum in which they may be seen to be engaged in a meaningful dialogue regarding common concerns. It gathers poems of fifty-one poets and one liberation movement, FRELIMO (Front for the Liberation of Mozambique), written between 1945 and 1982, and deliberately emphasizes social commitment. The countries included are Angola, Botswana, Malawi, Mozambique, Namibia, South Africa, Zambia, and Zimbabwe.

The poems from Angola and Mozambique, former colonies of Portugal, were written in Portuguese and appear here in translation. With the exception of those written by Mazisi Kunene and Mudereri Kadhani, the rest were written in English. The two poets mentioned translated their own poems into English, and I would like to suggest that an element of translation may be involved in the composition process when a nonnative speaker decides to write in a borrowed language.

It must seem ironic and paradoxical to Westerners that African poets adopt metropolitan languages for some of their writing. This is a result of the ethnic narcissism of the colonial masters, who denigrated African languages and equated civilization with acquisition of a European language and culture. The colonial versions of the metropolitan languages were pervaded by a lexicon of violence, insult, command, and order, which made them instruments in the debasement and dehumanization of the colonized people. One of the African poets' tasks has been to wrestle the impure tongues into submission in order to cleanse and purify them into appropriate vehicles for their literature. This has been possible because they have danced with these languages since the fifteenth century, when European adventurers first landed on the coast of sub-Saharan Africa. It has been a long war dance, with unwilling partners, in which oral and alphabetic literary modes have fused into new syncretic forms.

Those who are concerned about where this collections of African poetry fits in with Western literary tradition must bear in mind that it is in the nature of syncretic literature to partake of both worlds, although it may or may not retain the original constituent traits in their pure form. This anthology has its place in world literature, of which Western literature is only a small part, because the poems deal with universal human concerns and values. This poetry is not, however, a mere extension of Western literary traditions; instead, it reflects in its major themes and attitudes the contentious relationship between Europe and Africa.

The major recurrent themes in this anthology are Negritude; protest against colonial domination and apartheid; anger and bitterness over oppression; alienation and conflict; the return to cultural roots; national pride; community and kinship transcending ethnic and racial lines; love, hope, the beauty of the land, and the pathos of the human condition. These thematic elements bind the poetry in a common regional culture although the poems themselves reflect the diverse traditions of each country. These are poems of vision and possibility, pointing to a world of higher spiritual values, the ideal that directs the quest for collective self-realization, wholeness, and freedom in the face of lives fragmented and distorted by oppression and tyranny.

A shared vision also justifies the inclusion of poems by Costa Andrade, Antonio Jacinto, and José Luandino Vieira, three white Angolan poets in this anthology. The first two were born in Angola, where they grew up among their fellow Africans, assimilating and internalizing African values, attitudes, and styles to the extent that their poems have appeared in anthologies meant for black Africans only. Vieira, although born in Lagoa do Furadouro, Portugal, emigrated to Angola as a child and lived in such slums of Luanda as Makulusu, Kinaxixi, and Ramalho, among poor blacks, whites, and *mestiços*, or mulattoes. Except for Andrade, who was exiled to Brazil by the Portuguese authorities, these poets shared prison cells with fellow African political prisoners in the notorious Tarrafal Prison in the Cape Verde Islands for their anti-imperialist activities.

In Central and Southern Africa, more than in West and East Africa, there is a strong relationship between poetry and politics, a fact that explains the general outlook of this anthology. Most Angolan and Mozambican poets were forged and shaped in the heat of the struggle against Portugal, their common oppressor. This accounts for the thematic, stylistic, and tonal similarities in their poetry. Other poets from this region were also politically active; they, too, have never been exempted from oppression. Because of their dual activities, the poets of Central and

Southern Africa have frequently been persecuted, driven into exile, or detained in their own countries, where their poetry has been censored and banned from circulation.

This anthology is evidence that their poetry has transcended all efforts to suppress and contain it.

ANGOLA

to our lands
red with coffee
white with cotton
green with maize fields
we must return
　　—Agostinho Neto

I N   T H E I R   P O E T R Y, Angolans are not merely protesting, but also inciting to and voicing revolt against an unjust colonial regime. In their themes, styles, and tones the poems are almost indistinguishable from those of Mozambique. The similarities in expression correspond to their experiences under the same colonial master, Portugal, which necessitated the adoption of identical means of protest and resistance. Both conducted protracted guerrilla warfare against Portugal. The poets share, not only the Portuguese language, which distinguishes their work from that of English-speaking Central and Southern Africa, but also the same dehumanizing process and enslavement, hardship, political imprisonment, torture, and exile.

The dominant themes in the poetry, found also in Mozambican poetry, are not really different from those of South African, Zimbabwean, and even Malawian poetry. They give expression to the suffering, imprisonment, exploitation of African laborers, massacres of innocent civilians, alienation, cultural conflict, Negritude, the loss of and the quest for human dignity, return to cultural roots, love of the people and their land, hope for freedom and justice in a multiracial society, the armed struggle, and their people's triumphs. In their need to identify themselves with the oppressed, the poets have adopted such figures as the contract worker, the migrant laborer, the stevedore, and the slum dweller as major symbols for their poetry. The same symbolic figures feature regularly in Mozambican poetry especially, and in South African poetry under different names.

Stylistic parallels exist between Angolan poetry and the rest of the poetry in this collection, though it has greater affinities with Mozambican poetry in its simplicity of diction, pared-down lines, vivid imagery, and clear, accessible language. Angolan poets often use incremental repetition of word or phrase, alliteration, assonance, variation of line length to simulate movement, and the rhythms and beat of drums. In many instances they incorporate lines from African songs, chants, and folk tales. However, they are more experimental in their use of language, in their fusion of colloquialisms, slang, and formal language, than their Mozambican counterparts. They also freely use snatches of conversation, street talk, calls and vendors' cries, onomatopoeic words, sometimes stretching vowels to capture echoes or sounds of trains, refrains, and questions.

Many of the poems are directed at particular audiences; they are addressed to mothers, friends, brothers, sisters, lovers. They are conversational and written in a communal voice, which is a mark of the oral tradition. As such, there is a great range of tones. Agostinho Neto, for example, can be defiant, firm, exhortative, imperative, and urgent, but he frequently assumes an affectionate tone when addressing his kinfolk, always instilling hope and courage in them, inspiring them to struggle against evil, as does his Mozambican kinsman Marcelino dos Santos. Some of these poems voice vehement rejection of Portuguese domination and strong indignation against colonial atrocities in angry, condemnatory, and uncompromising tones, which is characteristic of Mozambican poetry, too.

Almost ten years have elapsed since Angola became independent, and already some of the themes of that country's poetry—including Negritude, protest against colonial domination, and oppression by foreign masters—are waning or have almost completely disappeared. Yet, while undertaking national reconstruction, these poet-politicians have had to fight a new aggressor, South Africa. Thus, for some time perhaps, we shall still hear of suffering and protest, against apartheid, in a condemnatory tone and a unified voice, in defense of their nation.

COSTA ANDRADE

Costa Andrade was born in 1936 in Lepi, Huambo, in Angola. He studied architecture in Portugal and in Yugoslavia, and he has also lived in Brazil and Italy. In Lisbon he was a leading figure in the Casa dos Estudiantes do Imperio from 1957 to 1961. During this time he was twice held for investigation by PIDE (the Portuguese political police). In 1961 he joined the MPLA (Popular Movement for the Liberation of Angola) and was sent to Brazil, where he worked as an architect and MPLA representative in São Paulo. From 1968 to 1974 he fought on the Eastern Front in Angola, and in November 1974 he was sent to the MPLA delegation in Huambo. In January 1976 he was appointed Director of the *Jornal de Angola*, the major daily newspaper in Luanda. He has published poems, short stories, essays, and criticism in several countries, and his poems have appeared in numerous anthologies. His publications include: *Terra de acacias rubras, Tempo angolano em Itália, Poemas, O Regresso e o Canto, Poesia com Armas,* and *O Caderno dos Herois.*

Fourth Poem

There are on the earth 50,000 dead whom no one
mourned
  on the earth
    unburied
      50,000 dead
whom no one mourned

A thousand Guernicas and the message in the
  brush strokes of Orozco and
      de Siqueiros

it had the dimensions of the sea, the silence
spread across the land

as if the rains rained blood
as if the coarse hair was grass many meters high
as if the mouths condemned
in the very moment of their 50,000 deaths
all the living of the earth

There are on the earth 50,000 dead
whom no one mourned

no one . . .
the mothers of Angola
    died together with their sons.

Translated by Michael Wolfers. © 1979 Costa Andrade. Translation © 1979 Michael Wolfers. By permission of Heinemann Educational Books.

Augusto Ngangula

I want to see here
alongside this silent hero
of twelve years
those men who are so ardent
for the equality of men.

I want to see here
on this soil stained
with the blood of a twelve-year-old youngster
the mothers of the free children
of the same age.

I want to see here
alongside this tortured body
the clamor of those who cry out against war
here
alongside the brave heart
of such as die at the age of twelve
those who speak of tomorrow
and promise the distant future.

I want to see here
the men who know about space
and control the cosmic flights
and do heart transplants
and decode the electronics of sound
and sing to burst the eardrums
and paint good pictures
and argue the fine points of issues
in front of this ravaged corpse of a twelve-year-old.

Here
alongside this child
cut off at the age of twelve
I want to see oceans
lakes
palm groves
and paper toy boats.

Here
the weapons from all sources
promising solidarity
on the sure path
to life.

I want to see here
alongside the cold body of the smiling
twelve-year-old
children with pencils and exercise books
learning
to write just his name.

And purged at last
of these cliffs of anger
the day will be filled
with roundelays
on the evergreen youth
around the stone raised in remembrance.

Translated by Michael Wolfers. © 1979 Costa Andrade. Translation © 1979
Michael Wolfers. By permission of Heinemann Educational Books.
The poem celebrates the heroism of Augusto Ngangula, a twelve-year-old Angolan
boy beaten to death by Portuguese soldiers on December 1, 1968, for refusing to
reveal the location of his bush school, run by the MPLA.

ARLINDO BARBEITOS

Arlindo Barbeitos, a *mestiço* (a mulatto) was born on Christmas Eve in 1940 in Angola. He was educated there and in Portugal, which he left in 1961 to travel extensively in North Africa and Europe. In 1965 he settled down in West Germany in order to continue his studies in sociology, economics, and philosophy. In 1971, during the war in Angola, he returned there and taught in MPLA (Popular Movement for the Liberation of Angola) secondary schools in the liberated zones. Tuberculosis forced him to leave the country again the following year. He entered the graduate program in ethnology at the University of West Berlin, where he earned a Ph.D. degree. He returned to Angola in 1975 to become a professor at the University of Lobango. He has published two books of poetry: a volume of war poetry, *Angola Angolé Angolêma*, and *Nzoji* (Dreams).

A Man of Rain

a man of rain
lies dead on the ground of decayed leaves

perhaps only the birds
which appear to be building nests
in the ruins of houses made of clouds
can notice

a man of rain
lies dead on the ground of decayed leaves

Many Years Ago

Many years ago
there was a year
with such rats
that the rats ate the cats
and the men ate the rats

        Many years ago
        there was a year
        with such locusts
        that the locusts ate the corn
        and the men ate the locusts

Many years ago
there was a year
with such a drought
that the land ate the lakes
and the men ate the land

Translated from the Portuguese by Ronald Rassner. © 1984 by Ronald Rassner. By permission of the translator.

O Night Flower

o night flower
where all dew is lost

your eyes
are not stars
are not hummingbirds

your eyes
are immense chasms

where in the darkness
an entire past is hidden

your eyes
are immense chasms
where in the darkness
an entire future is formed

your eyes
are not stars
are not hummingbirds

In the Forest of Your Eyes

in the forest
of your eyes
only night is seen

in the night
of the leopard
only eyes are seen

in the dawn
of the night
only your eyes are seen
and
in your eyes
of the leopard
only the forest is seen

EMANUEL CORGO

Emanuel Corgo (pseudonym of Eurico Manuel Correia Gonçalves) was born in Luanda, Angola, where he attended secondary school before studying law in Portugal. He deserted from the Portuguese colonial army and went for military training to Korea. In 1970 he began service in the Popular Movement for the Liberation of Angola (MPLA)'s second political-military region, in Cabinda. On August 1, 1974, in the first formal commissionings, he signed the proclamation of FAPLA as Northern Front Political Commissar and Column Commander. He was killed in Luanda on May 27, 1977, a victim of a counterrevolutionary coup against the Angolan government. At the time of his death he was Head of the Personnel Section of FAPLA's General Staff and a member of the Council of the Revolution, provisionally the highest legislative body in Angola. His poems appeared in newspapers and anthologies, but much of his writing was unpublished in his lifetime.

Against Negritude

The prison fetters ate into our flesh
    in the holds of the slave ships
    on the cotton plantations
    or under the coffee trees
but we do not seek reparations for the past

The whip scored our naked backs
    in the coal mines
    on the cane plantations
    or when we said NO
but we are not prisoners of history

The *palmatoria* bit into our hands
  because we had not paid their tax
  or because we did not accept
  the hunger with which they taxed us
but the day of victory draws near

Every day they spit on the blackness of our skin
  in Africa
  in Europe
  and in America
but we shall not for this hate men

Today the people demand that we fight
  with weapons in hand
  and that we struggle
  and that we struggle
  once twice or a thousand times
until there is built a better world.

Translated by Michael Wolfers. © 1979 Emanuel Corgo. Translation © 1979
Michael Wolfers. Reprinted from *Poems from Angola*. By permission of Heine-
mann Educational Books.
Palmatoria (Portuguese) is a wooden spoon with holes in it used by Portuguese
colonialists to beat people's palms; the impact draws flesh into the holes, causing
it to burst.

VIRIATO DA CRUZ

Viriato da Cruz was born in 1928 in Porto Amboim, Angola. He was one of the founders of the Vamos Descobrir Angola (Let Us Discover Angola) movement and also of the Popular Movement for the Liberation of Angola (MPLA), which he served as Secretary General. He became a dissident and was expelled in July 1963 for indiscipline. He was Editor of *Mensagem* (Messages), a left-wing literary journal, which launched many of the currently important Angolan writers. A number of his major articles were published in European cultural journals. A member of the Afro-Asian Writers Committee, he published one book, *Colectanea de poemas, 1947-1950*. He died in China in 1973.

Black Mother

Your presence, mother, is the living drama of a race
drama of flesh and blood
which Life has written with the pen of centuries.

Through your voice

    Voices from the cane plantations,
      the paddy fields, the coffee farms,
        the silk works, the
    cotton fields
    Voices from the plantations in Virginia
    from farms in the Carolinas
    Alabama
      Cuba
        Brazil
    Voices from Brazilian sugar plants
      from the tonga drums, from the
      pampas, from factories,

Voices from Harlem District South,
   voices from slum locations,
Voices wailing blues going up the
   Mississippi, echoing from railroad wagons.
Voices weeping with Carrothers' voice
   "Lord God, what evil have we done"
Voices of all voices in the proud voice
   of Langston
in the beautiful voice of Guillén . . .

Through your back

   Gleaming backs beneath the world's strongest suns
   Gleaming backs making fertile with their blood
     working soft with their sweat
     the world's richest soils
   Gleaming (ai, the color of those backs . . .)
   Gleaming backs twisted on the torso
     hanging from the gallows, struck down by Lynch
   Gleaming (ah, how they gleam, those backs)
   Revived with Zumbi, raised up with Toussaint
   Gleaming backs
   they gleam, they gleam, drummers of jazz
   they break, they break the fetters of the soul
   escape soul on the wings of music
   . . . of sunlight, of the sun, immortal, fecund
     and beautiful.

Through your lap, mother

   Rocking these other people
   spoiled by the voice of tenderness
   and fed on your sustaining milk,
     the good of poetry
     of music, of rhythm and gracefulness,
   sacred poets and wise men . . .

These people have no sons
for these which are born like wild beasts,
self-generated, different things
are rather the sons of disgrace:
the hoe is their plaything
slave labor—their recreation . . .

Through your eyes, mother,

I see oceans of grief
lit by the setting sun, landscapes,
violet landscapes
dramas of Cain and Japheth.
But I see as well (oh, if I see . . .)
I see as well how the light robbed from your
    eyes now glows
demoniacal temptress—like Certainty
glittering steadily—like Hope
in us, your other sons
making, forming, announcing
the day of humanity
THE DAY OF HUMANITY.

Translated by Margaret Dickinson. © 1972 Viriato da Cruz. Reprinted from *When Bullets Begin to Flower*. By permission of East African Publishing House Ltd.

James David Carrothers was an Afro-American minister / poet born in Cass County, Michigan, in 1869. The line quoted is from his poem "At the Closed Gates of Justice" ("To be a Negro in a day like this— / Alas! Lord God, what evil have we done?")

Zumbi was the last ruler of the Quilombo of Palmares in Brazil, 1695.

ANTONIO JACINTO

Antonio Jacinto was born in 1924 in Luanda, Angola. He was a pioneer in the movement for cultural nationalism in all its phases and has had an enormous influence on other Angolan poets. He was arrested by PIDE (the Portguese secret police) as an MPLA (Popular Movement for the Liberation of Angola) militant and condemned to fourteen years in the Tarrafal Prison, in the Cape Verde Islands. In 1972 he was allowed to live in Lisbon, where he worked as an accountant; he escaped from Portugal the following year and joined the active ranks of the MPLA. In November 1975 he accepted an appointment as Minister of Education and Culture in the first government of independent Angola. In November 1976 he became Secretary of the National Council on Culture, and in December 1977 he was elected a member of the Central Committee of the MPLA–Workers Party at the first congress of the MPLA in Luanda. His poems have appeared in many anthologies and have provided lyrics for some of Angola's most popular songs. He has published *Colectanea de poemas*.

Letter from a Contract Worker

I wanted to write you a letter
my love
a letter to tell
of this longing
to see you
and this fear
of losing you
of this thing which deeper than I want, I feel
a nameless pain which pursues me
a sorrow wrapped about my life.

I wanted to write you a letter
my love
a letter of intimate secrets
a letter of memories of you
of you
your lips as red as the tacula fruit
your hair black as the dark diloa fish
your eyes gentle as the macongue
your breasts hard as young maboque fruit
your light walk
your caresses
better than any that I find here.

I wanted to write you a letter
my love
to bring back our days together in our secret haunts
nights lost in the long grass
to bring back the shadow of your legs
and the moonlight filtering through the endless
palms,
to bring back the madness of our passion
and the bitterness of separation.

I wanted to write you a letter
my love
which you could not read without crying
which you would hide from your father Bombo
and conceal from your mother Kieza
which you would read without the indifference
of forgetfulness,
a letter which would make any other
in all Kilombo worthless.

I wanted to write you a letter
my love
a letter which the passing wind would take

a letter which the cashew and the coffee trees,
the hyenas and the buffalo,
the caymans and the river fish
could hear
the plants and the animals
pitying our sharp sorrow
from song to song
lament to lament
breath to caught breath
would leave to you, pure and hot,
the burning
the sorrowful words of the letter
I wanted to write you.

I wanted to write you a letter
but, my love, I don't know why it is,
why, why, why it is, my love,
but you can't read
and I—oh, the hopelessness—I can't write.

Translated by Margaret Dickinson. © 1972 Antonio Jacinto. Reprinted from *When Bullets Begin to Flower*. By permission of East African Publishing House Ltd.
Macongue is henna, or red dye made from its leaves.
Maboque is the wild orange.

Monangamba

On that big estate there is no rain
it's the sweat of my brow that waters the crops:

On that big estate there is coffee ripe
and that cherry-redness
is drops of my blood turned sap.

The coffee will be roasted,
ground, and crushed,
will turn black, black with the color of the
    contratado.

Black with the color of the *contratado*!

Ask the birds that sing,
the streams in carefree wandering
and the high wind from the inland:

    Who gets up early? Who goes to toil?
    Who is it carries on the long road
    the hammock or bunch of kernels?
    Who reaps and for pay gets scorn,
    rotten maize, rotten fish,
    ragged clothes, fifty angolares,
    beating for biting back?
    Who?
    Who makes the millet grow
    and the orange groves to flower?
    —Who?
Who gives the money for the boss to buy
cars, machinery, women
    and Negro heads for the motors?

Who makes the white man prosper,
grow big-bellied—get much money?
—Who?

And the birds that sing,
the streams in carefree wandering
and the high wind from the inland
will answer:
—Monangambeeee . . .

Ah! Let me at least climb the palm trees.
Let me drink wine, palm wine
and fuddled by my drunkenness forget

—Monangambeeee . . .

Translated by Margaret Dickinson. © 1972 Antonio Jacinto. Reprinted from *When
Bullets Begin to Flower*. By permission of East African Publishing House Ltd.
Monangamba is a contract worker hired during colonial days as a laborer on the
Portuguese coffee or cotton plantations.
Contratado is also a contract laborer.

The People Went to War

On the matting
bathed in the blackness
with which smoke cuts off the sun
Mother Lamba,
lost in present memories of her absent husband,
puts ointment on her son

Kaianga's wife is weeping

Kaianga has gone to war, Kaianga has gone to war

In the solitary township
lights and shadows play silently between the huts
children sleep
old people dream
dogs sit panting
flies buzz round the dunghill
and from the roofs, threads of water drip
—life affected by the absence of men—

The sun burns an open question

The people have gone to war, the people have gone to war
when will they come back?
and no wing cuts the empty sky

Kaianga has gone to war, Kaianga has gone to war
I don't know if he'll come back

The people have gone to war, the people have gone to war
I do know: the people will come back.

Translated by Margaret Dickinson. © 1972 Antonio Jacinto. Reprinted from *When Bullets Begin to Flower*. By permission of East African Publishing House Ltd.

Punishment for a Wayward Train

That wayward train
goes by
goes by always with its force
    ué ué ué
    hii hii hii
te-quem-tem te-quem-tem te-quem-tem
    the wayward train
    goes by

At the windows many people
    ai bô viaje
    adeujo homéé
lovely young ladies
quitandeiras with their red kerchiefs
some carry sugar cane to sell in Luanda

hii hii hii
    that stake car carries oxen
            múu múu múu
it has another
like that car of oxen
the train carries people
    many people like me
full of dust
people are like oxen
people bound to contract

There are oxen who die on the trip
but the black doesn't die
he sings like a child
    *"Mulonde iá Késsua uádibalé
    uádibalé uádibalé . . ."*

That wayward train
alone on the tracks
goes by
  goes by
without respect
          ué ué ué
leaving smoke behind
         hii hii hii
te-quem-tem te-quem-tem te-quem-tem

Translated from the Portuguese by Ron Rassner and Alexander Caskey. Translation
  © 1984 by Ronald Rassner. By permission of the translator.
Mulonde iá Késsua uádibalé uádibalé uádibalé is a line from a Kimbundu folk song.

Antonio Jacinto   27

AGOSTINHO NETO

Agostinho Neto was born on September 17, 1922, in Kaxikane Village, Catete District, Icolo e Bengo region, some forty miles from Luanda, in Angola. He qualified as a medical doctor in Lisbon and returned to practice in his own country. He was associated with Viriato da Cruz's movement for the rediscovery of Angola's indigenous culture. In 1960 he was elected President of MPLA (Popular Movement for the Liberation of Angola); in the same year he was arrested (for the third time) by PIDE (the Portuguese political police) agents in his private hospital in Luanda and detained in Lisbon. But in 1962 he escaped, aided by members of the democratic resistance movement. Back in Angola, he continued to lead the struggle until Angola gained its independence in 1976, becoming the first president of the new nation. Many of his poems were smuggled out of prisons, and are the best known of all Angolan poetry. They form the basis of many popular songs. Widely published in anthologies and journals, his poems have been translated into many languages, including English, Chinese, French, Italian, Romanian, Russian, Serbo-Croat, Spanish, and Vietnamese. His publications include: *Quatro Poemas de Agostinho Neto, Poemas, Con Occhi Asciutti* (With Dry Eyes), a bilingual Portuguese-Italian volume, translated by Joyce Lusso, *Sagrada Esperança*, published in English as *Sacred Hope*. He died in 1979 in a Moscow hospital after a long illness.

Farewell at the Hour of Parting

My Mother
   (all black mothers
   whose sons have gone)
you taught me to wait and hope
as you hoped in difficult hours
But life
killed in me the mystic hope

I do not wait now
I am he who is awaited

It is I my Mother
hope is us
your children
gone for a faith that sustains life
Today
we are naked children in bush villages
schoolless children playing with a ball of rags
in the sands at noon
we ourselves
contract workers burning lives in coffee
                              plantations
ignorant black men
who must respect the white man
and fear the rich
we are your children
of the black neighborhoods
beyond the reach of electric light
drunken men falling down
abandoned to the rhythm of the *batuque*
                              of death
your children
hungry
thirsty
ashamed to call you Mother
afraid to cross the streets
afraid of men
We ourselves

Tomorrow we shall sing anthems to freedom
when we commemorate
the day of the abolition of this slavery

We are going in search of light
your children Mother
   (all black mothers
   whose sons have gone)
They go in search of life.

Translated by Marga Holness. © 1974 Agostinho Neto. Reprinted from *Sacred Hope*. By permission of Tanzania Publishing House.
Batuque is a dance.

The Marketwoman

The marketwoman
   Strong sun
and the marketwoman in the shade
of the *mulemba.*

—Orange, my lady
a nice little orange!

Light plays in the town
its burning game
of brightness and shade
and life plays
in worried hearts
its game of blindman's buff.

The marketwoman
who sells fruit
sells herself.

—My lady
orange, nice little orange!

Buy sweet oranges
buy from me too the bitterness

of this torture
of life without life.
Buy from me the childhood of the spirit
this rosebud
that did not open
start still impelled to a beginning.

—Orange, my lady!

I exhausted the smiles
with which I cried
I no longer cry.

And there go my hopes
as did the blood of my children
mingled with the dust of roads
buried on plantations
and my sweat
soaked in the cotton threads
which cover me
As effort was offered to
the security of machines
the beauty of tarmac roads
of tall buildings
comfort of rich gentlemen
happiness dispersed in towns
and I
became a part
of the very problems of existence.

There go the oranges
as I offered myself to alcohol
to anaesthetize myself
and gave myself up to religions
to desensitize myself
and stupefied myself to live.

I gave all.

Even my pain
and the poetry of my naked breasts
I gave to the poets.

Now I myself am selling me
—Buy oranges
my lady!
Take me to the markets of Life
My price is only one: Blood.

Perhaps selling myself
I possess myself.

—Buy oranges!

Translated by Marga Holness. © 1974 Agostinho Neto. Reprinted from *Sacred Hope*. By permission of Tanzania Publishing House.
Mulemba is a sycamore tree.

Western Civilization

Tins fixed to stakes
driven in the earth
make the house

Rags complete
the intimate landscape

The sun piercing the cracks
awakens the inhabitant

After twelve hours of slave
labor

Breaking stones
carrying stones
breaking stones
carrying stones
in the sun
in the rain
breaking stones
carrying stones

Old age comes fast

A reed mat on dark nights
enough for him to die on
thankfully
and of hunger.

Translated by Marga Holness. © 1974 Agostinho Neto. Reprinted from *Sacred
Hope*. By permission of Tanzania Publishing House.

Kinaxixi

I liked to sit
on a bench at Kinaxixi
at six o'clock of a very hot evening
and stay there ...

Someone would come
perhaps to sit
to sit beside me

And I would see the black faces of people
going up the alleyway
leisurely
expressing absence in the hybrid Kimbundo
of their talk

I would see the weary steps
of serfs whose parents were also serfs
seeking here love there glory
beyond drunkenness in every alcohol

Neither happiness nor hate

When the sun went down
they would light the lamps
and I
would go off aimlessly
thinking that our life is simple after all
too simple
for he who is tired and has to walk on.

1950

Translated by Marga Holness. © 1974 Agostinho Neto. Reprinted from *Sacred Hope*. By permission of Tanzania Publishing House.
Kinaxixi is the public marketplace in the city of Luanda, Angola.
Kimbundo (Kimbundu) is the language of the Umbundu people of southern Angola.

Friend Mussunda

Here I am
Friend Mussunda
here I am
with you

with the firm victory of your joy
and of your consciousness

O ió ḳalunga ua mu bangele
O ió ḳalunga ua mu bangele-lé-lelé . . .

Do you remember?

The sadness of those times
when we used to go
to buy mangoes
and regret the fate
of the women of Funda
our songs of lamentation
our despair
and the clouds in our eyes
Do you remember?

Here I am
Friend Mussunda
My life I owe to you
to the same devotion, to the same love
with which you saved me from the embrace
of the boa
to your strength
which transforms the destiny of men

To you Friend Mussunda
to you I owe my life

And I write poems you cannot follow
do you understand my anguish?

Here I am
Friend Mussunda
writing poems you cannot follow

It was not this
we wanted, I know

But in spirit and intelligence
we are!

We are
Friend Mussunda
we are
inseparable
and still advancing to our dream

On my path
and on your path
hearts are beating rhythms
on bonfire nights
feet are dancing on stages
of tropical mystiques
The sounds do not fade from hearing

O ió kalunga ua mu bangele . . .

We are.

Translated by Marga Holness. © 1974 Agostinho Neto. Reprinted from *Sacred
   Hope*. By permission of Tanzania Publishing House.
O ió kalunga ua mu bangele / O ió kalunga ua mu bangele-lé-lelé (Oh! it was
   destiny that created you) is a children's play song.

We Must Return

To the houses, to our crops
to the beaches, to our fields
we must return

To our lands
red with coffee
white with cotton
green with maize fields
we must return

To our mines of diamonds
gold, copper, oil
we must return

To our rivers, our lakes
to the mountains, the forests
we must return

To the coolness of the *mulemba*
to our traditions
to the rhythms and bonfires
we must return

To the marimba and the *quissange*
to our carnival
we must return

To our beautiful Angolan homeland
our land, our mother
we must return

We must return
to liberated Angola
independent Angola.

Alijube Prison, Lisbon, October 1960

Translated by Marga Holness. © 1974 Agostinho Neto. Reprinted from *Sacred Hope*. By permission of Tanzania Publishing House.
Quissange is an Angolan musical instrument that is strummed.

AIRES DE ALMEIDA SANTOS

Aires de Almeida Santos is an Angolan poet about whom little is known. His work has appeared in Portuguese-language anthologies.

When My Brothers Come Home

When my mother shall see my brothers
And embrace them
We'll go to live
On the Catete road
       We'll have to build with our own hands
       A small house
       Well made
       Where we'll all go to live.
       It will be red
       And covered all over with thatch.

       The work will be easy
       For the clay is already stained
       With so much, so much blood

       It has had so much time to run—
There will be a garden as well
With roses and bougainvilleas
       That will be easy
       For even if the rains come late
       It will be watered
       By the tears
       That all our eyes have shed.

When my mother shall see my brothers
And embrace them
We'll all go to live
On the Catete road

And we'll eat dried fish
And drink *Quissangua*
Brought from Bié
And we'll sleep on grass matting
Soothed by the light wind
Blowing on Musseque
      We shall rest
      From the long road traveled
      We shall rest
      Ready for the longer road ahead

Oh, when my mother shall see
My brothers and embrace them
It will be small, our well-built house
      (although I have millions of brothers)

When my mother shall see my brothers
And embrace them
We'll go and sweep
Away the ashes of those who went before

And sing
Spreading our joy
On the mountainside
Through the drifted sand,
In the valleys,
On the banks of streams,
And up by the springs
      We must sing!

Ah, when my mother shall see my brothers
And embrace them
A fire will burn
The height
Of each furrow
And the light
Of each star
Will be greater

Mother, listen to your son

DON'T WAIT, MOTHER

THEY ARE COMING, SWIFTLY . . .

Translated by Margaret Dickinson. © 1977 Aires de Almeida Santos. Reprinted
from *When Bullets Begin to Flower*. By permission of East African Publishing
House Ltd.
Quissangua is a type of Angolan beer.
Bié is a district in Angola.

ARNALDO SANTOS

Arnaldo Santos was born in 1936 in Luanda, Angola. He is a short-story writer and poet whose work has been published in Portuguese-language journals and anthologies. He has published two books: *Fuga* and *Quinaxixe*.

Season of Blood

> The flowers on the coffee trees
> I
They are no longer white
the latest flowers on the coffee trees

They are no longer white

A red dew has settled from dawn
and the droplets were pulsing on the flowers
like hearts torn from their chests

> Season without sky
> II
And then a new day was born
like a flame
a river ablaze

And in the current I was swept up
like a constellation of cries

> bone shards
> convulsions

With my startled eyes
white in a skyless season
    inhuman
With my gesture a weary farewell
and the suicidal vertigo of my intention:
    to tear out my bowels
        and hurl them in the face of this season.

Uije, April 1961

Translated by Michael Wolfers. © 1979 Arnaldo Santos. Translation © 1979 Michael Wolfers. Reprinted from *Poems from Angola*. By permission of Heinemann Educational Books.

LUANDINO VIEIRA

Luandino Vieira was born José Vieira Mateus da Graça, in 1935, to a peasant family in Portugal, but he grew up in the poor townships of Luanda, Angola. He was made an Angolan citizen in 1976 in recognition of his work with the MPLA (Popular Movement for the Liberation of Angola) during the struggle for independence. Detained in 1959 for a month, he was again arrested in 1961 and was sentenced to fourteen years in prison. After a period of detention in Luanda, in 1964 he was transferred to Tarrafal, in the Cape Verde Islands. In 1972 he was allowed to live under restricted residence in Lisbon, where he worked for Ediçoes 70, a publishing house. He returned to Angola after the overthrow of the fascist government in Portugal in 1974, and became Director of Programs for People's Television, which started experimental transmissions in November 1975. In 1977 he was appointed Director of MPLA's Department of Revolutionary Orientation. He is the best-known Angolan prose writer and won literary prizes for his work even while in prison. Although his work was banned at the time, clandestine editions were issued by daring publishers in Portugal. He has published two novels, six collections of short stories, and individual stories and poems in journals, newspapers, and anthologies. His *A Vida Verdadeira de Domingos Xavier* was also published in English.

Song for Luanda

The question in the air
on the shore
on the tongue of everyone
        —Luanda, where are you?
Silence in the streets
Silence on the tongues
Silence in the eyes

—Hey
sister Rose the fishwife
can you tell?

—Brother
I can't tell
have to sell
rush around the city
if you want to eat!

"Lu-u-nch, choose your lu-u-u-nch
sprats or mackerel
fine fish, fine fi-i-i-sh"
—You then
Mary, market mammy
selling wild orange
breasts of wild orange
shouting
bouncing
your feet skipping
on rust red roads
all day long?
"Wild orange fine wild orange
sweeter than sweet"

—Brother
I can't tell you
time is running short
if I want to make a sale!

Half-caste Zefa
body up for sale
rouge on her lips
earrings of brass
and that brass's smile
offering her body

—built like a house!
Her body's up for sale
it's been around
by night and day.
              —Luanda, where are you?

Half-caste Zefa
built like a house
earrings of brass
she's good for a lay
with someone who'll pay
—a girl's gotter eat!

—Newspaper fellow
Luanda, where are you?
The ancient houses
the rust-red clay
even our ballads
bulldozed away?

Nippers in the streets
children's forfeits
"now you're caught"
tricks and treats
swallowed by asphalt?

—All the sisters
fishwife Rose
market mammy Mary
not forgetting you
half-caste Zefa
and your earrings of brass
              —Luanda, where are you?

With a smile
punnets on the ground
fruit and fish
sweet wild orange
hope-filled eyes
sure touch of hands
sister Rose the fishwife
market mammy Mary
Zefa the half-caste
—whether your clothes be shoddy
or gaudy
or bawdy
they give away your heart:
—Luanda, you are here!

Translated by Michael Wolfers. © 1979 Luandino Vieira. Translation © 1979
Michael Wolfers. Reprinted from *Poems from Angola*. By permission of Heine-
mann Educational Books.

BOTSWANA

This is my native land
My real native land
I know every tree or bush by its name
I know every bird or beast by its name ...
                    —Albert G. T. K. Malikongwa

ALBERT MALIKONGWA is the oldest (born 1930) of a group of
new Botswana poets searching for their voices. A characteristically
wordy poet, in the poem "A Protest from a Bushman (Masarwa),"
he boldly attempts to marry utterance with a persona who, seemingly
preoccupied with the physical aspects of his native land, seeks to re-
connect himself to the things dear to him, to redefine himself in the
context of his landscape, and to correct a distorted image of himself im-
posed upon him by others. He is not, unlike the elite, searching for an
identity; he has lost none. Rather, he is protesting against the forces that
alienate him from his land, that denigrate his culture, that subject him to
torture, suffering, and constant humiliation.

Thematically, this poem belongs to the group that embodies expres-
sions of love for the native land common to the poetry of Angola and
Mozambique. In sentiment and defiant tone it also belongs with black
South African poetry, and in its architectonic method of cumulatively
building statement upon statement, it approaches traditional oral poetry,
in which the various attributes of the praised object are given in inter-
related statements. It is also one of the few poems in the collection that
employ a dramatis persona.

The Masarwa man reveals his cosmic consciousness as he re-creates,
in simple, direct, Biblical language (Psalm 50), a world we have hitherto
been unaware of. He names his world, describing it lovingly, possessively,
passionately, confidently: the birds whose names he knows by heart, the
trees, the bush, the flowers, the moon, the stars, the rainbow, and the
wind. We recognize him as the Khoi-khoi hunter in Namibian Mvula

Ya Nangolo's "Hunter's Song," who has roamed the land hunting, dancing, and staying wherever he chooses. He is the free spirit who resists and rejects circumscription and proscription. Malikongwa's poem achieves dramatic vigor and verve from common speech, and its incantatory style approaches the Whitmanesque style of the Mozambican poet José Craveirinha. He, too, lists, catalogues, and uses incremental repetition of plain direct statements.

The Masarwa combines affectionate tones, in which he describes and reclaims his native land in ways reminiscent of Angola's Agostinho Neto and Mozambique's Marcelino dos Santos, and defiant tones, in which he protests against dispossession, denigration, and second-class citizenship in his own land in the manner of many South African poets. But Botswana, the Masarwa's native land, is an independent country, and Malikongwa's unflinching poem serves to alert his own countrymen to certain vital problems they may have overlooked.

ALBERT G. T. K. MALIKONGWA

Albert G. T. K. Malikongwa was born in 1930 in Mayebe, Nswazwi village, near Francistown, in Botswana. After attending St. Joseph's College, Khale and Mariazell Training School, and Roma College in Botswana, he taught in Zimbabwe, from 1954 to 1967. He then joined the Botswana Public Service and, in 1968, studied public administration for a year at the University of York, in England. He works for the government of Botswana, and has published playscripts and poems in Southern African journals.

A Protest from a Bushman (Masarwa)

This is my native land
My real native land
I know every tree or bush by its name
I know every bird or beast by its name
I care not that I am poor
I have lived in this land
And hunted all over these mountains
And have looked at the skies
And wondered how the stars
And the moon and the sun and the
Rainbow and the Milky Way rush
From day to day like busy people
I have enjoyed this life
The light in the stars
The lilt in the music or songs
The joy in the flowers
The plumage of the birds
The charm in women's breasts
The inward warmth and rich vitality
The distant music of cowbells
All these lightened the burdens of my sorrow

I have nothing outside this body
I have neither a house nor property
I roamed where I liked and hunted where I chose
And have enjoyed the bounce of youth
And stayed where I chose
I have danced in the sun
I have danced in the wind
I have danced around the fire place
But now and I say now there is
A swelling crescendo of sorrow
That makes goose-pimples on my body
There is no more joy in me
I live in sick apprehension
Life is tremulous like a waterdrop on a mophane tree
My body is wrinkled, my hair grey
The talk is Bushmen everywhere
I am called a "no body"
A race of ragged filthy people
Who cannot clean their floors
Whose blanket is the firewood
Who spit and sneeze freely everywhere
Whose bodies smell of root-ointment
Or like a cowhide soaked in the river water
My countrymen call me names
I am torn between life and death
Propped between freedom and slavery
My tears glide in pairs down my cheeks
My hands shake because of old age
I am no more than a refugee
A loafer they say
Yet others loaf too whilst other men work
It is true I do not worry for lunch
As birds do not worry for theirs too
To me the delights of knowledge
And the pomp of power are anathema
Life is tremulous like drops

Of water on a mophane leaf
My countrymen eat, drink and laugh
I and my fellow men and women sleep under trees
In caves or open ground
We starve, we can no longer hunt freely
Life is a scourge, a curse
It is tremulous like a drop of water on a mophane leaf.

MALAWI

Mute necklaces of stone, mist-nuzzling mountains
Deep green lush grass feeding on springs of blood
And silent ambers, a memory of raging flames of fire . . .
—Frank Mkalawile Chipasula

MOST OF THE Malawian poetry in this anthology constitutes a reaction to postcolonial oppression, and in that sense it differs from the poetry of neighboring Mozambique, South Africa, and Angola. It demonstrates a heightened awareness of the social and political contradictions in this country ruled single-handedly by a black dictator and lifetime president. For fear of reprisals, the pervasive censorship, and possible detention, the poets cannot adopt a public stance and voice, unlike the poets involved in the freedom struggles in the former Portuguese colonies and in Rhodesia and South Africa. Although some of the poets are old enough to have experienced colonial oppression, they prefer to deal with the harsh realities of contemporary Malawi. Consequently, they tend to write as individuals, in private and personal voices, about personal experiences, with which, however, many people identify.

The themes of Malawian poets—arbitrary detention, mass murder, the tyranny, despotism, and hero-worship of the iron-handed dictatorship, and the sad, yet farcical, paternalism that masquerades as benevolent liberalism—are not unique. They are not only voicings of these harsh realities, but also calls to the populace to confront these issues.

Stylistically, the poems show a greater preoccupation with technique, in the service of concealing the protest element, and with metaphorical statement and imagery than most of the other poets in this collection, who depend on direct accusative statement. This obsession with irony, ambiguity, understatement, subtlety, euphemism, and myth has sometimes resulted in absurdities and facile obscurity, but it has, in a large measure, paid recognizable dividends.

Jack Mapanje is a poet of multiple voices well orchestrated into a harmonious symphony. Like a chameleon, a pet symbol of his, he assumes and plays various roles, performing to an enthusiastic audience which shares in his quizzical look at the world around him. His poems often question such pretentious terms as "development," "modernity," "progress" and the slogans shouted by so-called patriots. In his best poems, he combines a somber tone with metaphorical language in carefully balanced and controlled forms, the sound patterns of which are ordered by repetition of line or word, as in Malawian song. In some poems, such as "The New Platform Dances," Mapanje's power derives from direct rhetorical questions and cumulative statements that are conjured up to constitute the utterance of a particular character, thus revealing his experimental attitude toward Malawian speech. Many of his poems are short, and their economy of language results in condensed lines, vivid imagery, and a finished quality. He can be cynical, sardonic, threatening, though he is careful to keep his voice low, preferring to puzzle out the blatant contradictions in his country from a quiet distance. Like Steve Chimombo, he attempts to versify Malawian folk tales and myths, elevating such characters as chameleon, frog, and other folkloric figures into symbols. He also transforms folk histories of tyrants and despots in a way that enables him to comment on present realities with great subtlety.

Mythmaking is a source of power for Lupenga Mphande, too. His poetry flourishes on irony, understatement, euphemism, and indirection, and marries wit to a prophetic and apocalyptic vision. A good example of his method is "The Dwarf of the Hill Caves," which wittily allegorizes an interesting, yet extremely bizarre example of irrationality in contemporary Malawian political history. Mphande's style is contemplative and strongly descriptive, yielding carefully ordered, long, fluid lines, which pulsate with the rhythms of nature. He has a keen eye and sharp ear, and his poems teem with sensuous images of cicadas, mosquitoes, hills, ridges, valleys, trees, grasslands, streams, and brooks. His experiments with full rhyme and half and near rhyme often produce the effect of spontaneous movement and sound in rural landscapes, which he loves to paint in words. Of all the Malawian poets, he is perhaps the only one who has faithfully and lovingly rendered the beauty of rural Malawi, exemplifying the intimacy many of us feel with the land. In some poems, he juxtaposes the beauty of the land with the violence perpetrated on innocent peasants by their insensitive masters ("The Victim"), producing a shocking effect. His most chillingly prophetic poem is "When the Storms Come," which masks his extreme anger at the myopia of the corrupt and despotic leaders, but, as usual, he withdraws into the background, content to perform his role as a visinary or seer.

Steve Chimombo's myth-laden poem "Four Ways of Dying" counsels indirection as a viable stylistic and strategic device in dealing with the country's realities, using the crab's movements, a river's meandering, the chameleon's camouflage, the mole's underground life metaphorically to suggest alternatives to direct action, confrontation, and commitment in a country where even to *think* is subversion. His dilemma regarding the appropriate language a poet must adopt to obtain the password that might enable him to elude the vigilant censors while simultaneously bearing the message of life to the people is not uncommon to writers in his country, to writers under siege.

Nothing can be published in Malawi without the prior approval of the Censorship Board; consequently, the fear of censorship and detention has hindered the steady literary growth that was envisaged in the early seventies. To date, only three writers have published volumes of poetry. After my pioneering book, *Visions and Reflections* (National Educational Company of Zambia, Lusaka, 1972), eight years elapsed before Dr. Felix Mnthali published *When Sunset Comes to Sapitwa* (National Educational Company of Zambia, 1980), followed by his *Echoes from Africa* (1981) and *Beyond the Echoes* (1982), both published by Amulefi Publishing Company, in Buffalo, New York. Although Dr. Jack Mapanje's *Of Chameleons and Gods* was published in 1981 by Heinemann Educational Books, in London, the Malawi Censorship Board has not yet approved it for circulation in Malawi. It is also very doubtful that my second book, *O Earth, Wait for Me* (Ravan Press, Johannesburg, 1984), will ever reach the country.

Censorship and the leadership's intolerance toward criticism may also have been responsible for silencing some of the older poets. David Rubadiri, the country's best-known poet for many years, now living in exile, has not published a book of his poems, though he has been anthologized all over the world. Dr. James Chipasula, who won a first prize in the Anglo-American Corporation's Poetry Competition in Chingola, Zambia, in 1965, has not been heard from since. And Dr. Guy C. Z. Mhone, whose poems appeared in various U.S. journals in the sixties and ten of whose poems were included in Keorapetse Kgositsile's anthology *The Word Is Here: Poetry from Modern Africa* (Doubleday, 1973), seems to have abandoned poetry altogether.

Despite all the adverse conditions under which Malawian poets must operate, they refuse to be silenced totally, and some of the most active continue to deal with suffering, violence, arbitrary detention, humiliation, the quest for self-conscious manhood and womanhood, despair, and also the hope for a better future, themes that link their poetry to that of the rest of the region.

INNOCENT BANDA

Innocent Banda was born in 1948 in Zimbabwe, but of Malawian parents. He was educated at Soche Hill College and Chancellor College, University of Malawi, from which he received a B.Ed. He also earned an M.A. in linguistics from the University College of North Wales. He has taught in secondary schools and worked as an assistant editor of a national magazine in Blantyre. He has been an assistant lecturer in English at the Polytechnic, University of Malawi and at Chancellor, and now teaches at Nyadire Teachers College in Mtoko. An established playwright, his *The Lean Year*, broadcast in 1969 by the Schools Broadcasting Unit of the Malawi Broadcasting Corporation, is among the earliest plays by Malawian writers. He was a runner-up in a BBC playwriting competition and appears in James Gibbs's *Nine Malawian Plays*. His poems have appeared in journals and anthologies in Malawi and abroad.

Malawi

Malawi, your secret flame
burnt itself out torching the settlers
with the unrestrained zeal of
aging grey-haired Presbyters
purging our land of its true patriots
like old gods piled on the pyre,
as we embraced new synthetic ones
elevated on shaky stilts
on the squeaky platforms
kissing Leza's long fiery
beard with impunity.
They lacerate our land with the steel
hair of their fly whisks
(we weep at the deep lesions and scars)
as a red sea of party women

sings national hallelujahs:
Malawi, your faint fire
shimmers still in the rice valleys,
in the ripening highland tobacco,
on the mad lake flaring
with its snarling waves like cobras.
Malawi—a gem
glistening, stuck in the mire of avarice,
the rekindled Liunde fire overwhelms
the church candles as we tune up
the drums to wake up the sleeping,
the flames consuming the false citadels.
A new fire smolders like the flame
of a purifying forge where
the hammer pounds the tapering
angry spearhead.
Malawi, your name means tomorrow!

Liunde is the initiation camp for Chewa boys in central Malawi and eastern Zambia.

Where Is the Fruit

Where is the fruit
the milk
the honey
in this land of promise?

I have crossed your Jordan
many times
walked the desert
thirsty
hungry
wishing for manna . . .

I invested sleep
keeping vigil
zokoma ziri mtsogolo
when I lived this life
and I'm ready to go
zokoma ziri mtsogolo
there is no point
when I cross the second Jordan
I will hear again
zokoma ziri mtsogolo

Where is the fruit
in this land you promised?

Zokoma ziri mtsogolo is Chewa for "the good things are to come."

Lindedi Singing

More than once I have heard
The lindedi singing in the night.
In the valley I have heard
The owl warning sleeping folks.

And then
Amidst all quietness
I have heard
A human cry of sorrow,
And without warning
I have tasted
The salt of my twin fountains.

Stand up at daybreak
And see the beauty of the valley.
Go down
And feel the peace
Overflooding the valley.
But beneath that green
Sleep-laden figures
I have seen
Clothed in sorrow
While behind the doors
I have heard men curse
Their brothers
As they squeezed
Their lives out.
The clouds shed their water
When they can't hold it,
Like a cup that overflows,
Or eyes that shed tears
When the heart is full of sorrow.
These blades of grass
Bring to my memory
The tear-laden lashes
That I saw
On the night she went away.
In the wind
I hear her still.
Now as I sit in the sun
The lindedi sings
And the owl hoots.
I see them coming
On their merciless mission
The crouching
Tigers of darkness
Bloodthirsty
Lions of the night.
I see them

Chasing her soul;
They tore her heart
And sucked her blood.
        Was it devilish?
Oh! that these very men
        We eat with
        May in the night
        Fall upon us!
Terror has wedded horror.
        In the village
        These blades of grass
        With drops of dew
Bring to my memory
        The tear-laden lashes
        that I saw
On the night she went away.
        In the wind
I hear her cry still.

A lindedi is a Malawian bird.

May Bright Mushrooms Grow

May bright mushrooms grow
Where
Crimson blood flowed
And
Where the poor fall
May the rich grow tall
Grinding the wounds
Of poverty

That There Should Be Laughter

For Mothers Day, Malawi

Dear Mothers
You have long bent your backs
Dancing in the perpetual carnival
Your gratitude
Goes on and on till pain
Grows glands in our throats
As we hopelessly watch you waste away.

Will you not go to the well
Or gather under the muula tree
To pound the empty mortars you abandoned?
Or in the young rays of a new morning
Throw your heads back and laugh
At the spineless men of the day?

If you compose a new song today
For us, ask only one thing:
That there should be laughter
The laughter that says
All is well again in the village
Where children wait
For the carnival to break up.

1982

STEVE CHIMOMBO

Steve Chimombo was born on September 4, 1945, in Zomba, Malawi. He was educated at Chancellor College, University of Malawi (B.A.), the University of Wales (T.E.F.L.), the University of Leeds (M.A.), and Teachers College, Columbia University (Ed.D.). He is Senior Lecturer in English and Head of the English Department at Chancellor. He has published short stories, essays, and poetry in Malawian and overseas journals. His first full-length play, *The Rainmaker*, was published in 1978, and a new play, in Chewa, *Wachiona Ndani*, is to be published.

Four Ways of Dying

The celebrants chanted
To the reluctant martyrs-to-be
We would have a blood sacrifice!

The Crab's response:
I crawl
        in my shell sideways
                backwards
                forwards
Avoid
        direct action on public matters
        confrontation
        commitment
Meander
        to confuse direction or purpose
                meaning
                sense

Squat
        to balance the issues
        weigh
        consider

The Chameleon's answer:
Until I have exhausted my wardrobe
Lost my dye to a transparent nothingness
Free of reflection, true to my image
I'll match my colors with yours
Snake my tongue out to your fears
Bare my teeth to puncture your hopes
Tread warily past your nightmares
Curl my tail round your sanctuaries
Clasp my pincer on your veins
To listen to your heartbeat.

The Mole's descent:
Wormlike I build in the entrails of the earth
Fashion intricate passages and halls
Tunnel utopias and underground edens
Substitute surface with subterranean vision
Level upon level of meaning of existence
As I sink downward in my labyrinth
To die in a catacomb of my own making.

The Kalilombe's ascent:
The gestation and questionings are over
I'm restless with impatient foetuses
Bellyful with a profusion of conundrums
My pilgrimage takes me to the cradle
The njave tree, the lie-in of man's hopes
I grit my teeth, grab the slippery surface
And hoist myself up the nation's trunk
On the topmost branch I have momentary
Possession of eternity whirling in the chaos

With the death song floating from my lips
I fling myself down on Kaphiri-Ntiwa rock
As multivarious forms of art and life
Issue out from the convulsions
Of the ruptured womb
And thus I die.

Kalilombe is a figure in a Malawian creation myth.
Kaphiri-Ntiwa is a mountain in Malawi.

FRANK MKALAWILE CHIPASULA

Frank Mkalawile Chipasula was born on October 16, 1949, and is a Malawian. He studied at Chancellor College, University of Malawi for three years, received a B.A. from the University of Zambia, and was a Fellow in Writing at Brown University, from which he received an M.A. in creative writing in 1980. He has been a Teaching Fellow in the Department of Afro-American Studies at Yale University, and while there earned an M.A. in Afro-American studies (literature). Currently a teaching assistant in the English department at Brown, he is a candidate for a Ph.D. degree in English literature. He was a founder and an organizer of the Writers Group at Chancellor College. His book *Visions and Reflections* was a pioneer volume of poetry in English by a Malawian writer. He was the editor of *A Decade in Poetry*, an anthology of Zambian poetry. His poems and essays have appeared in journals and anthologies both in Malawi and abroad.

A Love Poem for My Country

For James

I have nothing to give you, but my anger
And the filaments of my hatred reach across the border.
You, you have sold many and me to exile.
Now shorn of precious minds, you rely only on
What hands can grow to build your crumbling image.

Your streets are littered with handcuffed men
And the drums are thuds of the warden's spiked boots.
You wriggle with agony as the terrible twins, law and order,
Call out the tune through the thick tunnels of barbed wire.

Here, week after week, the walls dissolve and are slim,
The mist is clearing and we see you naked like
A body that is straining to find itself but cannot
And our hearts are thumping with pulses of desire or fear
And our dreams are charred chapters of your history.

My country, remember I neither blinked nor went to sleep
My country, I never let your life slide downhill
And passively watched you, like a recklessly driven car,
Hurrying to your crash, while the driver leapt out.

The days have lost their song and salt.
We feel bored without our free laughter and voice.
Everyday thinking the same and discarding our hopes.
Your days are loud with clanking cuffs
On men's arms as they are led away to decay.

I know a day will come and wash away my pain
And I will emerge from the night breaking into song
Like the sun, blowing out these evil stars.

A Hanging

Zomba Central Prison

His pendulous body tolled
its own death knell from the rope
yet refused obstinately
to die, clinging desperately
to the last thread
of his condemned life.

That morning oh!
his body sang until it could not
stand its own song;
like a guitar it hummed
and they could not but listen, stunned.
Every part of his body
opened its mouth and sang
death songs, Orphic heart songs,
shrill and sweet pent-up
songs of freedom or sad and solemn
as the national anthem.

The heartstrings raised their harp
in a flood of insistent rhythm
and a slow drumming dance:
All his blood stood up and sang,
twisting towards the throat.
All the silent mouths raised their voices
and cried out their chorus.
No one could gag or stop the prison
walls from singing;
No one could muzzle or shield the ringing
echoes of Zomba mountain.
And the whispering pines on Queen's Point,
witnesses to the sordid deed,
raised their frosty mourning.

His heart was a cube of golden light,
a nest of incense where weaver-
birds had made their welcome permanent,
weaving a wall of thin silken tears
that sang with the lips of broken earth,
rolled waves, resistant and durable wind.

From every pore on his body a river of song
or wail sprang and poured out.
His feet opened out like dark petals and chirped;
his fingers bloomed and plucked his heartstrings.
The song twined into the *makako* and jammed it;
the looped noose would not close, numbed.

Being political, he was not entitled
to the miraculous luck of the criminals.
So they called in the prison doctor
to administer the *coup de grâce*.
He stabbed the chest with a thick
syringe and pumped the poison
into the heart with orgasmic release.

The heart made a sudden excited leap,
missed only one deceptive beat
and resumed its journey as usual.
Slowly he turned into a deep emerald green
and covered the whole country.

Like a stone he would not die.
They summoned a hard-core life prisoner,
placed a rock hammer in his hand
and ordered him to locate the victim's heart.
He bashed in the chest completely
and left a wide yawning gap. Not murder
technically, only routine execution.

Then a waterfall of blood! There was no one
that the blood did not touch and baptize.
Pilate searched vainly for water
to cleanse his hands of the *business*.

The song gushed out in a steady jet.
The body tolled its final knell
and then momentarily froze, then in a futile
move to cross the dark river before him,
he spread out his legs and kicked
and tried to rip the darkness that cloaked him.

Then . . . ah, this is *it*.
The final parting moment, the end, the last
wisp of breath escaping from his gaping mouth
again with the song rising like smoke.
He wanted the last swing, the final
expression of his freedom, arrested and preserved

before the sandbags dragged his compressed body
into the dark hole, into total oblivion.

© 1982 Frank Chipasula. Reprinted from *Contact II*.
Makako is the gallows.

Those Makheta Nights

I heard the crude gin sobbing
in the Lactogen milk-can tots
in the rusty complaints of the creaking
bolt, hinges and the flapping iron
roofs yanked and toyed by the wind
like goat-skin bellows sharpening a flame
and the men mourning over it
strange winds neighing painfully
in a drop of the opaque Chibuku beer
trapped, suffocated in a decorated cardboard
packet to be shaken among
the long tongues of *kholoboyi* lamps.

The long dry fingers of the winter plucked
the banjo and guitar wires, twisted our learned bellies
till they groaned, screamed with mustered bitterness
echoing the mysterious sobs of the gin's "head"
flaming from the mud floor, intoxicated paper-thin
babies, their ribs mere accordions stretched
by the violent hands of perpetual hunger,
wailed their own dirges from their mothers' backs
bulging eyes loaded with itchy sleep
wakeful at midnight, watching their mothers' flesh
melt in the discordant music of banged
empty cans, the violins of injured winds
in the blue gum trees guarding the fleshpots
and the scratchy groans of the *Simanje-manje* bulls
charging heatedly from the grooved wax.

We held those dejected, sweat and smoke-filled
nights intimately by their elusive wasp waists
fast changing into serpents, flames consuming
the dense desire and passion thick as mist.

Here the Party's knobkerries could not reach us
under the mask of irrational and forgetful gin
and its hidden daggers, our trusted efficient weapons;
Out of those nights shall emerge
the blade of the flame that will rend the dark cloak!

© 1982 Frank Chipasula. Reprinted from *Cencrastus*.
Makheta is a slum township in Blantyre, Malawi.
Chibuku is a commercially brewed beer popular with workers and lower-class town
    dwellers in Central Africa.
A *kholoboyi* ("call boy") is a lamp made from a can and a wick; it is used by
    workers.
Simanje-manje is neo-traditional, modern South African music popular in Central
    Africa.

Frank Mkalawile Chipasula   71

JACK A. MAPANJE

Jack A. Mapanje was born of Yao and Nyanja parents in Kadango Village, Mangochi District, southern Malawi. After obtaining a diploma in education at Soche Hill College, University of Malawi, he taught in Malawian secondary schools for a number of years, then entered Chancellor College, University of Malawi, to obtain a B.A. degree. He was Lecturer in English at the University of Malawi, but left for the University of London to complete his Ph.D. degree in linguistics, which he did in 1982. He now teaches oral literature and linguistics at Chancellor. A founder and one-time director of the Writers Group, he now also edits *Kalulu*, a journal of oral literature. His poems have been published in African and European journals. He has edited an anthology of Malawian poetry and has published a volume of his own poetry, *Of Chameleons and Gods*.

A Marching Litany to Our Martyrs

In the name of our dear brothers dead
Are we really marching to these tin drums
Rattling the skeleton beat of heroic
Bones long laid asleep?

The planes that dropped white emergency papers

Do we really halt to revere perplexed
Elders now only shades shaking and
Tossing synthetic calabashes of Chibuku
Beer which numbs their brains?

Those stooges' cars and houses fire-gutted

Have we really about swung to these
Frantic maxi-skirts slit to thighs
Opening to whispers and caresses of
Midnight breezes and coins?

And the barricades and bridges shattered

Do we salute the squealing laughters
Of the broken hearts in their shells
Clicking their crumpled tin cans of
Goat urine to their bungled dreams?

What of the tear gas and the bullets on their heads?

Do we now troop past the skeletal mothers
Before their sons' burial mounds weeping
With broken bowls of rotten weevils
And shards of sour brew for their libation?

And those bitter tears and the blood that gushed

In the name of our growing bellies,
Batons, buggers and bastards rife,
Let us revel in parades, lowering the emblem
Of precious bones long laid asleep.

Amen!

3 March 1971

The martyrs of the title are the men, women, and children gunned down on March 3, 1959, in Malawi during the struggle for freedom. Martyrs' Day is observed every year now in Malawi.

The New Platform Dances

Haven't I danced the big dance
Compelled the rains so dust could
Soar high above as when animals
Stampede? Haven't I in animal
Skins wriggled with amulets
Rattled with anklets
Scattered nervous women
With snakes around my neck
With spears in these hands
Then enticed them back
With fly whisk's magic?
Haven't I moved with all
Concentric in the arena
To the mystic drums
Dancing the half-nude
Lomwe dance?
Haven't I?

Haven't my wives at mortars sung
Me songs of praise, of glory,
How I quaked the earth
How my skin trembled
How my neck peaked
Above all dancers
How my voice throbbed
Like the father-drum
I danced to?
Haven't they?

Now, when I see my daughters writhe
Under cheating abstract
Voices of slack drums, ululate
To babble-idea-men-masks
Without amulets or anklets

Why don't I stand up
To show them how we danced
Chopa, how IT was born?
Why do I sit still
Why does my speech choke
As though I have not danced
Before? Haven't I
Danced the bigger dance?
Haven't I?

Lomwe are the people of the Thyolo and Mulanje districts of southern Malawi and
parts of Mozambique.
Chopa is a Lomwe ritual dance performed in connection with rain-making, fer-
tility, gods, power, and in celebration of harvest.

Before Chilembwe Tree

1

Didn't you say we should trace
your footprints unmindful of
quagmires, thickets and rivers
until we reached your nsolo tree?

Now, here I seat my gourd of beer
on my little fire throw my millet
flour and my smoked meat while
I await the second coming.

2

Why does your mind boggle
Who will offer another gourd
Who will force another step
To hide our shame?

The goat blood on the rocks
The smoke that issued
The drums you danced to
And the rains hoped for—

You have chanted yourselves hoarse
Chilembwe is gone in your dust
Stop lingering then:
Who will start another fire?

John Chilembwe (1871(?)–1915), American-educated Malawian minister, led the 1915 uprising against the British colonialists in what was then Nyasaland; now immortalized as the first genuine Malawian revolutionary.

On His Royal Blindness Paramount Chief Kwangala

I admire the quixotic display of your paramountcy
How you brandish our ancestral shields and spears
Among your warriors dazzled by your loftiness
But I fear the way you spend your golden breath
Those impromptu, long-winded tirades of your might
In the heat, do they suit your brittle constitution?

I know I too must sing to such royal happiness
And I am not arguing. Wasn't I too tucked away in my
Loincloth infested by jiggers and fleas before
Your bright eminence showed up? How could I quibble
Over your having changed all that? How dare I when
We have scribbled our praises all over our graves?

Why should I quarrel when I too have known mask
Dancers making troubled journeys to the old mines
On bare feet and bringing back fake European gadgets

The broken pipes, torn coats, crumpled bowler hats,
Dangling mirrors and rusty tin cans to make their
Mask dancing strange? Didn't my brothers die there?

No, your grace, I am no alarmist or banterer
I am only a child surprised how you broadly disparage
Me shocked by the tedium of your continuous palaver. I
Adore your majesty. But paramountcy is like a raindrop
On a vast sea. We should not wait for the children to
Tell us about our toothless gums or our showing flies.

Kwangala is a Yao word meaning to dance frantically.

When This Carnival Finally Closes

When this frothful carnival finally closes, brother
When your drumming veins dry, these very officers
Will burn the scripts of the praises we sang to you
And shatter the calabashes you drank from. Your
Charms, these drums, and the effigies blazing will
Become "the accomplices to your lie-achieved world"!
Your bamboo hut on the beach they'll make a bonfire
Under the cover of giving their hero a true traditional
Burial, though in truth to rid themselves of another
Deadly spirit that might otherwise have haunted them,
And at the wake new mask dancers will quickly leap
Into the arena dancing to tighter skins, boasting
Other clans of calabashes as the undertakers jest:
What did he think he would become, a God? The devil!

GUY C. Z. MHONE

Guy C. Z. Mhone was born of Malawian parents in 1942 in Zambia, where he was raised. He received his early education in Zambia, Zimbabwe, and Malawi, and earned a B.A. in economics at Dartmouth, and an M.A. and a Ph.D. in economics at Syracuse. He has been a professor at the State University of New York at Oneonta since 1972, and a Visiting Lecturer at the New School for Social Research in New York City. His book, *The Political Economy of a Dual Labor Market in Africa: The Copper Industry and Dependency in Zambia, 1929–1969*, was published in 1982. His poems have been published in many journals in Africa and the United States since the late nineteen-sixties.

The Chisizas I

Promoted, kicked upstairs
To a nowhere somewhere
We celebrated, rejoiced.
And now back
To a transcendental
Nowhere
They celebrate, rejoice.

Rejoice?
We called them Du, Yatu.
Rejoice?
Dear God!
Or maybe, is it
Compromising timidity
Of a beleaguered peasantry?

Like time's timelessness
Our ancestors' agelessness

Du and Yatu live
In one with us,
Haunting the living
With an ancestral message
"HE must go"
Purgatorio? Inferno?

It behooves us
Yah, to do
What Yatu, Du
Craved for.

Winter 1967

Dunduzu K. Chisiza was the first Malawian Parliamentary Secretary to the Minister of Finance, organizer of Blantyre Economic Symposium 1962, and author of *Africa What Lies Ahead*. He died in a mysterious car accident in 1962. Yatuta Chisiza, brother of Dunduzu, was the first Minister of Home Affairs. He opposed Banda openly in the 1964 Malawian Cabinet Crisis and led a guerrilla group that engaged the Malawi Army successfully, inflicting heavy casualties. He was shot dead by a wounded soldier while removing identity papers from those killed.

A Lament to My Mother

I was sung to you
In me your first born
And now I see on my face
A wrinkle like your dimple
On your elbow/ and now
Here I stand sinking in my dirt
But still the reason for your dimple
I will remember/ black mother/

You cried me on a wrinkleless, black face
And bore a dimple on your elbow
Even though the spirals in your hair
Moistened by your silent tears
I still cannot see in the morning.
Black mother, I still am
One of the soil.

Summer 1968

FELIX MNTHALI

Felix Mnthali was born of Malawian parents in 1933 in Selukwe (now Shurugwe), Zimbabwe. He was educated in Lesotho and Canada, where he obtained his Ph.D. in English. He joined the faculty of Chancellor College, University of Malawi, in 1969, and was at one time its Provost (Deputy Vice-Chancellor). He has chaired "Literature Magazine" on Radio Malawi since its inception, establishing himself as a literary critic of national repute. He has published three volumes of his poetry. After a period in detention, he was reinstated Reader in English and Dean of the School of Arts at Chancellor. He is now Professor of English at the University of Botswana, in Gaborone.

Resurrection: Fragments

I

Visions of the world beyond these walls recede;
aching ribs detach themselves from
cement floors and dusty blankets—
those indifferent shrouds to
martyrs without a cause

Perched on a bucket for faeces
freshly cleansed of its night soil
I brood on the simplicity of man
while all around me stand
throngs of faces
faces in knots of ten or more
glued to the vibrations of other faces

      wrinkled
      wizened
      pained

beyond their years and hanging on bodies
that once looked human clutching with iron hands
filthy plates of lukewarm porridge
without sugar and without salt

11

Around some orators crowds always gather
like rain clouds around invincible peaks;
men gaze as if in a trance
at the deliberate gestures
the professorial jokes
the Lumumbist beard
the patched trousers
and the tattered coat.

We have been entombed
by all that is ugly in this land
and in lands like this
and yet
and yet here within walls
as inspiring as the shaft of a grave
eloquence blooms like mushrooms in the rainy season
and irony and satire
cut deeper than blades of steel.
We are buoyed by each other's wit
and the stubborn faith
of men adrift
on uncharted waters
for between this tomb
and the sun and bloom
of the world beyond these walls
yawns infinity

Perched on my cylindrical chair of rusty metal
which has served generations of prisoners before me
day in and day out, night and day

I brood on the infinite littleness of man
while all around me stand
throngs of faces
faces in knots of ten or more
glued to the vibrations of other faces

      wrinkled
      wizened
      pained

beyond their years
and hanging on bodies that once looked human . . .
    I brood on man "in his littleness of man"
    and before me float the mists of antiquity
    and the jungle to which man
"in his littleness of man"
so very easily and at times so gladly returns
canceling with a pen
and in a minute of peevishness
what took lives and aeons to build.
The tower with the armed guard,
the barbed wire, the open sewage
where men eat
while others defecate
were solid and real
and neither saints nor madmen
could bring them down
with a mere trumpet—

it is the walls within me
that are beginning to cave in . . .

    III

Suddenly, all too suddenly,
the yard is charged with the pantomime of war
hands go limp

with salutes and
the return of salutes:
the Commandant is expected
no, it is only his second-in-command . . .

Suddenly, all too suddenly
the roll call of salvation
begins . . .
Then as if from miles away
a trumpet blasts forth
this litany of my colonial heritage:
"Dr. Felix Winfrid James Mnthali"
    Bwaaanaaa!
    and the prison yard applauds
    perhaps the mystery
    perhaps the courage
    most certainly the comedy
    surrounding this resurrection
    this other side of my scar.

        IV

To walk into the sight of flowers
and sniff the breezes from Lake Chirwa and Zomba mountain
Can man ask for more?

We are clutching the rags of time
and trying to come to terms
with bits of selves
shelved on the day of arrest.

Antonina

Red, green, yellow, pink—
the bars along the road to Liwonde
go dizzy
with the footwork of possessed dancers;
on the tall stools and in "reserved" chambers
man-eating idols sniff the tenderized bodies
of warm Mona Lisas from village cradles.

Dancing like the wind
we echo the wail of Antonina
mourning her lovers
who have been looked for
and reported "taken"
dreaming of plays they had written
of monographs on literature and culture
of research on the Viphya Plateau
while all around them
men lie squeezed in fives and sixes,
a paltry sacrifice
to the parody of dawn.

Why must shadows follow us everywhere
spreading a pall over drinking sprees
rebuilding nightmares
of thugs and serpents in three-piece suits?

Why must the tears of Antonina
in this blinding fog
of fermented grain and deafening din
lead us only
to the knock that rapes our dreams
at four o'clock in the morning
and not at all
to the beauty of dawn?

Does the traveler return
when horizons fade and mists expand?
Does he flee from shadows
and curse his stars
for losing themselves
in the murky galaxy
of minor gods?

And why must shadows
in this unique land
among a gifted people
follow us everywhere:
from the cry in the maternity ward
through the sobs and tears of Antonina
to the numbness of guarded gates
and the wailing walls of single cells?

The Riddles of Change

They settle like dew

over the crannies
and crevices of our lives;
they blow

through the corridors of power

They prevail over this land
like the *chiperoni*
across the highlands;

they are here to stay,
these riddles of change.

Left, right and center
like a "happening" in the West
barked hounds by the hundred
men clutching shovels and pickaxes

So, that was it!
their turn had come
those mandarins and tinkers
we no longer wanted

But what have we gained
from our evasions, oversights, omissions
monumental mendacities
calculated in tranquillity?

They speak of final solutions
as if
beyond good and evil
a mere lie could be final;
as if the riddles of change
massed across the land

did not whistle
through the corridors of power
and settle like dew
over the crannies
and crevices of all our lives!

Chiperoni is the southwest prevailing wind that brings cold air to Malawi from the
Indian Ocean from May to August.

The Beauty of Dawn

How easy it is here
to be
no longer at ease
among our own people
clutching their shadows!

The land reels
from the repeated blows
of what we did
and did not do—

Where we wrestled with the devil
and snubbed temptation
how we fasted
for forty days and forty nights
while praying for the dawn—

When you come to see us
you will be haunted
by the incantations
around our bonfire—
feathers shake our glory
in the noonday heat,
and spears and assegais
nod their assent
to the conquests that are sung.

How easy it is here
among our own people
to clutch and hug the rags of yesterday
and sing and dance for the dawn.

Waiting for the Rain

Blank faces smile and nod
above limp hands
clapping their automatic
soundless and unintended
welcome

It has been done, before, done
under every shade and color of sky
from overcast, dark red to very clear

The robust and sweating poor of our sort
clap hands, sing and ululate
for Land and Range Rovers
Mercedes-Benzes and Toyota Crowns
Six-O-Fours and Datsun B's
forerunners of forerunners
with multicolored flashlights
and whizzing sirens
on their rooftops

It's been done, before, done
this ululation of the dispossessed
for the tired smile
and the tired nod
tired and sad
from praying for the rain

LUPENGA MPHANDE

Born on May 12, 1947, at Thoza, in northern Malawi, he attended
Embangweni primary school, and then went to Mzuzu and Dedza
secondary schools. He obtained a B.A. degree in English and history
from the University of Malawi in 1972, and an M.A. degree in applied
linguistics from the University of Lancaster in 1979. He also holds an
honorary doctoral degree in literature. He is editor of *Odi*, a bilingual
journal of literature published in Malawi, and has co-edited an anthology
of short stories. He is a founder-member of the Malawi Writers
Workshop and a literary critic for the Malawi Broadcasting Corporation.
His works have been published in various journals in Africa and
Europe. He is a lecturer in language and communication at the
University of Malawi, and is now a Ph.D. candidate at the University
of Texas, Austin.

The Victim

Every day at home I watched the landlord flog his men and bellow
Curses at them: one day I saw how one lad straightened up in a last
   groan
Of showered pain as he fell off the haypile shot through the head
I saw how the landlord grinned and my feet flapped, my eyes
   watered;

As I walked through tall grass along a stream
I saw how the soil was pure, the banks still fair and green
I watched a herd stoop to pasture, their eyes glistening
And my heart throbbed faster, my spirits rose high and clear;

At the riverbanks I watched a mouse tossed downstream
And merge in the eddies still fighting, and my heart grew heavy
As he clung to a vibrating reed like a tattered flag
I saw how the current overpowered him

Downstream I came across an abandoned rusty rifle
In the arresting silence I slowly looked around, sweating,
Then, with a deep sigh bent down, picked up the heavy load,
And started climbing the hillside back to the farm.

Song of a Prison Guard

I see you, prisoner of Dzeleka,
From behind this hole in the door panel;
I lurk along the hum of cicadas and mosquitoes
In moonshades of maize stalks and banana leaves
And shadows of barbed-wire posts and farm ridges.
I hide behind this iron cleft, and peep
Into your cell like a Cyclops, unseen—
I am guard to this humid valley prison camp.

Your little room, prisoner of Dzeleka,
Will grow forever small, your life in the lurch to waste
And cluck at the wind; even at night I will keep you awake
With the dry double lock designed to lacerate your sleep.
Don't tell me the political layout of your crimes;
I only stoke up furnaces for those I receive to roast
In chilly cells, and whet the axe for the condemned
To throttle at the gallows like a chick with its head off—
I am the guard charged with executions.

Do you see that window up the cell wall,
Prisoner of Dzeleka? Of course it's too small and will forever
Grow smaller, but look out sometimes on fine days;
If you find it painful to see children at play, and
Watch the life you've so unwittingly deserted, then study:

Count threads in a cobweb, rate the beams in a ray from
The crack on the eastern wall at break of day
Study the ray that lingers on after nightfall,
Study the strands in a life that's lost its shadow, study . . .

And when you discover the beam-wave that relates to your pain
Hum in harmony with cicadas and mosquitoes in the shade,
Celebrate the merger of darkness with midnight, do a dirge
To gods of swamps and hill caves, take three steps forward
Then backward and swerve—left right right left—
Weather changes in circles, dawn ousts darkness . . . Tropical
Summers are hot, but your cell will be a cold, cold winter:
You'll live in that narrow room to the final night.
It's like a piece of thread on which our days hang,
To fall away, one after another, wasted.

The Dwarf of the Hill Caves

There lives a celibate of the hill at home.
One day in a frenzy he dreamed visions
of a race of magicians who could boost
his dwarfish poise and patched domain.

He hastily retired up into his hill caves
to revel in the cabala and evoke the mountain gods,
to reveal to the world their unique potency of
leaping fly whisks and yoghurt from gyrating maidens.

Sacrifices completed and libation poured to the hill gods,
off he went on a quest to the west, to dip the charmed
root into molds of the dinosaur and drink rat urine
in accordance with the whispers from his mountain patrons.

When he returned, infested with lice and maggots
and his bag bulging with foreign roots and charms
potent in wild dreams and fantasies of towering ambition,
the transformation was complete; people flocked to him

Spellbound, to revel and gyrate to the occult
of the hillside caves, while the little man of the hill
snatched and wrung their bodies for yoghurt ingredient
to add to his possessions, attain height and beat the dwarf.

When the Storms Come

In time
    the lake will surge
    tossing pots
    gullying the soil
    in mid-current red showers

I am the blank between the colors
I am the one that foresees the end

In time
    the storm will come
    flooding the shores
    plateaux and mountains will crumble
    to level in tribal conflagrations

I am the interspace between tongues
I am the one that foresees the end

In time
  the sea will wash away the stain
  leaving the gash putrefied
  and beyond cleansing

I am the blank between the colors
  the interspace between tongues
  the one who foresees the end.

DAVID RUBADIRI

David Rubadiri was born in 1930 in Malawi, but grew up mainly in Uganda, where he received his early education at Kings College, Budo and Makerere College, before entering King's College, Cambridge, where he took the English tripos. After being detained in 1959 during the state of emergency in Nyasaland, he returned to Cambridge and became an active broadcaster. He served as the first Malawian Ambassador to the United Nations and the United States until 1965, when he joined the faculty of Makerere University, in Kampala, Uganda. He is now professor of languages and social science education at the University of Botswana, Gaberone. He is the earliest Malawian poet to write in English, and his poems have been published in numerous anthologies and journals. He has also published a novel, *No Bride Price*, and co-edited an anthology, *Poems from East Africa*.

The Tide That from the West Washes Africa to the Bone

The tide that from the west
Washes Africa to the bone
Gurgles through my ribs
And gathers the bones
That clatter into clusters,
Rough and polished,
To fling them back destitute
To the desolate riverbank.

The tide that from the west
Tears through the heart sinews of Africa
Boils in my marrow,
Dissolving bone and sinew.

The tide that from the west
Washes the soul of Africa

And tears the mooring of its spirit,
Till blood-red the tide becomes
And heartsick the womb—
The tide that from the west
With blood washes Africa
Once washed a wooden cross.

Begging A.I.D.

Whilst our children
become smaller than guns,
Elders become big
Circus Lions
away from home.

Whilst the manes age
in the Zoos
that now our homelands
have become,
Markets of leftovers
   Guns are taller
   than our children.

In the beggarhood
of a Circus
that now is home,
the whip of the Ringmaster
cracks with a snap
that eats through
the backs of our being.

Hands stretching
in prayer

of submission
in a beggarhood
of Elders delicately
performing the tightrope
to amuse the *Gate*
for *Tips*
that will bring home
Toys of death.

Thoughts After Work

Clear laughter of African children
Rings loud in the evening;
Here around this musty village
Evening falls like a mantle,
Gracing all in a shroud of peace.
Heavily from my office
I walk
To my village,
My brick government compound,
To my new exile.
In this other compound
I would no longer intrude.
I perch over a chasm,
Ride a storm I cannot hold,
And so must pass on quietly—
The laughter of children rings loud
Bringing back to me
Simple joys I once knew.

Yet Another Song

Yet another song
I have to sing:
In the early wake
Of a colonial dusk
I sang the song of fire.

The church doors opened
To the clang
Of new anthems
And colorful banners.

Like the Beatles,
The evangelical hymns
Of conversion
Rocked the world and me.

I knelt before the new totems
I had helped to raise,
Watered them
With tears of ecstasy.

They grew
Taller than life,
Grimacing and breathing fire.

Today
I sing yet another song,
A song of exile.

MOZAMBIQUE

This is the time we were waiting for.

Ahead of us we see bitter hardships.
But we see also
our children running free,
our country plundered no more.
                    —Josina Machel

In our land
Bullets are beginning to flower.
                    —Jorge Rebelo

M o z a m b i q u e, like Angola, was one of Portugal's overseas plantation colonies, exploited for its workers and its resources, and suffering from the coercive means used to make Africans grow cotton, sugar, cashew nuts, and other cash crops for the benefit of the parent state. It is not surprising, therefore, that Mozambican poetry voices the people's protest against foreign domination in terms similar to those in Angolan poetry. A recurrent theme in the poetry of both countries is the plight of the migrant laborer, who, after being broken physically and spiritually in the South African mines, returns to more degradation, humiliation, and poverty in Mozambique. Other themes, by now familiar, are the fragmentation of family life, the distortion of African culture, alienation, Negritude, protest against forced labor and arbitrary arrest, violence, hate, death, the search for identity, dignity, and hope. As in Angolan poetry, the armed struggle is a major theme, especially in combat poetry and in the celebration of heroes and heroines who died in the war for the liberation of the country. These war dead often become symbols of the struggle and are eulogized in the poems.

Stylistically, these poets draw heavily upon oral traditions, especially protest and work songs and folklore. Like the work of Angolans, their poetry is marked by a fluidity and transparency achieved through the use of simple, clear, straightforward language, concrete diction, direct statement, and sparse yet lucid imagery. An exception is Craveirinha's work, which has a blend of realistic and surrealistic imagery that adds a nightmare aspect to the depicted scenes. The short, slightly repeated lines in some Mozambican poems give them added power, verve, and a rhythm akin to African song. Like Angolans, too, these poets adopt African stylistic techniques, such as call-and-response, incremental repetition, anaphora, alliteration, and epistrophe to re-create drum rhythms and sound patterns, and to establish emphasis and symmetry. Some also exploit onomatopoeic repetition of lines to re-create sounds of trains or drums. In translation, some of the repeated sounds, such as the harsh nasals of Portuguese in Craveirinha's "Black Cry," are lost, although the tone and mood sometimes come through in the repeated words.

This section also contains collectively composed poems, those by-lined "FRELIMO," the liberation movement that fought Portuguese rule in Mozambique. The concept of collaborative composition is unique in written African poetry and is associated with oral tradition. Although some of the poems use the first-person pronoun, they are written with a communal voice and express communal feelings and sentiments. Issued as New Year messages, and sometimes Christmas cards, during the war, they employ simple, graphic imagery, with direct statement to redefine values, to suggest new aesthetics, and to justify the war as well as strengthen the hope of triumph. These poems are valuable because they help us appreciate the humanity of fighting people, those who, in this instance, were usually called "terrorists" in the Western press. They are not functional only; they are love poems fostering feelings of brotherhood and sisterhood transcending tribal and racial lines and divisive colonial policies.

The tones range from the defiant, condemnatory, and indignant to the angry, emotional, and passionate, in the Negritude poetry of Noémia de Sousa and José Craveirinha, to the affectionate, in Jorge Rebelo's poems. In their vehement protest against Portuguese oppression and tyranny, their threatening and challenging tones sometimes surpass those of Angolan poetry.

Like Angola, Mozambique's sovereignty continues to be challenged by apartheid South Africa, which has unrelentingly attacked the territory for the last ten years. Poetry continues to be written in Mozambique; in fact, masses of verse are being churned out in schools, factories, and other places, and much of this is laced with slogans and expressions of solidarity with South African people in their struggle for freedom. Like their Angolan colleagues, they have jettisoned the theme of Negritude, which dominated their early poetry, but their handling of the revolutionary theme leaves a lot to be desired. One hopes that they will, following José Craveirinha's example, plow back into their native soil the incredible energy that fired both the armed struggle and their combat poetry, so that those bullets that began to flower on the battlefield may now bear fruit: a truly autochthonous poetry enriched by the Mozambican myths and music that have invigorated the country's famous sculpture.

JOSÉ CRAVEIRINHA

José Craveirinha was born on May 28, 1922, in Maputo, Mozambique. A journalist, he worked for the bilingual weekly *O Brado Africano* (The African Cry), *Notiçias,* and *Tribuna.* In 1966 he was arrested, tried, and held in Machava Prison, near Maputo, where he was subjected to constant torture for his work in African resistance groups and FRELIMO (Front for the Liberation of Mozambique). He is the leading Mozambican poet. His first book of poetry, *Chigubo,* was published in 1964. Other volumes of poetry were *Karingana ua Karingana* and *Cela 1.* His poems have been included in anthologies both in Portuguese and in English translation. He works in the Library of the Economy at Eduardo Mondlane University, in Maputo.

Black Cry

I am coal!
You tear me brutally from the ground
and make of me your mine, boss

I am coal
and you burn me, boss
to serve you forever as your driving force
but not forever, boss

I am coal
and must burn
and consume everything in the heat of my combustion

I am coal
and must burn, exploited
burn alive like tar, my brother
until no more your mine, boss

I am coal
and must burn
and consume everything in the fire of my combustion

Yes, boss
I will be your coal!

1960

Mamana Saquina

Mamana Saquina
in the cosmopolitan, the dazzling mirage of the town
still kept her magic charms within her heart
at the hour of mourning
João.

Mamana Saquina
still kept the train's image in her mind
tangled with a song of steel on steel
to the beat João-Tavasse-went-to-the-mines
João-Tavasse-went-to-the-mines
João-Tavasse-went-to-the-mines
João-Tavasse-went-to-the-mines
João-Tavasse-went-to-the-mines

(On that morning of gilded cashew leaves
João Tavasse went to sign up at the depot)

And Mamana Saquina
stayed at Chibuto on the land
with Mamana Rosalina and *cocuana* Massingue
with ten hectares
in which to sow and to bring to flower
the Concession's seed

Night and day
the soul of Mamana Saquina swathed itself in nightmare
and buried itself in ten hectares of flowering cotton

(And João Tavasse
never came back to the depot)

Belching steam the miners' train pulled out
and in the pistons a voice sang
João-Tavasse-went-to-the-mines
João-Tavasse-went-to-the-mines
João-Tavasse-went-to-the-mines
João-Tavasse-went-to-the-mines

And Mamana Saquina mourned her son
scratched maize from the ground
and achieved the miracle of one hundred and fifty-
five bales of cotton.

Translated from the Portuguese by Margaret Dickinson. © 1972 José Craveirinha.
Reprinted from *When Bullets Begin to Flower*. By permission of East African
Publishing House Ltd.
The depot was the District Commissioner's post, where potential migrant laborers
went to enlist for service in the South African mines.
Chibuto is a district in southern Mozambique.
Cocuana means granny.

Mamparra M'gaiza

The cattle is selected
counted, marked
and gets on the train, stupid cattle.

In the pen
the females stay behind
to breed new cattle.

The train is back from *migoudini*
and they come rotten with diseases, the old cattle
    of Africa
oh, and they've lost their heads, these cattle *m'gaiza*

Come and see
the sold cattle have lost their heads
my god of my land
the sold cattle have lost their heads.

Again
the cattle is selected, marked
and the train is ready to take away meek cattle

Stupid cattle
mine cattle
cattle of Africa, marked and sold.

Translated from the Portuguese by Margaret Dickinson. © 1972 José Craveirinha.
    Reprinted from *When Bullets Begin to Flower*. By permission of East African
    Publishing House Ltd.
Mamparra is a migrant worker newly returned from the mines of South Africa;
    also a fool.
Migoudini means the mine.

Ode to a Lost Cargo in a Ship Called *Save*

How many died in the holds?
Those who were there, and us.

I

The ship was large
The ship was large, but not large enough.
The holds were enormous
The holds were enormous, but not enormous enough.

The berths were many
The berths were many, but there were not enough.
And the cargo ship ran aground.

But the disciplined merchandise was in there
And when the great company boat ran aground
A cargo of khaki uniforms and golden buttons
Relinquished all.

But don't despair, mothers,
Don't be sad, fathers, friends and brothers,
Don't soak your white handkerchiefs with tears of good-bye,
Idyllic widows and saddened sisters,
The ship was safe
And the lost cargo was insured
On the salty erotic breasts of the sea.
Don't be sad, widows of mourning,
Don't despair, old ones, fathers, friends and brothers,
The company's damages were covered,
The shipowner arrived for three days
On the front page of the newspapers
And never came again.

Under the hatchways
The company's cotton was the insured cargo
And the cargo that had no history of escudos

Or no mention in the lists of the ship's inventory
Were the sons and brothers and sisters,
Black, white, Chinese and mulatto,
Widowers, unemployed, football players without contracts,
All of them now recruits and nearly soldiers
With photographs of the type you put in numbered passes,
Khaki jackets and yellow buttons,
Eyes devoid of metaphysical questions,
Mouths without dialectic,
Singers, unfortunately, of only Rock 'n' Roll,
All of them beautiful with youth, absurd and incoherent,
Almost men, setting off together for the destiny of shell sounds
Dressed in the same unkind uniform
Purple in its Portuguese heat for ammunition

II

Who cried out?
It was the cargo.
Who burned?
It was the cargo.
Who was it that exploded?
It was the cargo.
Who disappeared?
It was the cargo.
It was the cargo which consumed its strengths,
The last of the burned arms and burned legs
The last of the glassy eyes and the burned hands
The last of the cries devoured by the flames
The last marijuana in military service
The last of the Mozambicans in a hiatus of agony.

Oh! The cargo freed the strengths in all the holds.
Oh! The cargo freed the holds of the burdens of cotton and youth.
Oh! The Company's cargo freed itself to the undulant sound of the
    waves

And the breeze of the palm trees crying over the waters of
    Quelimane
With the hull biting the hard rocks under the sea
And the rhythm of the marvelous crowd of living people on the
    decks,
The cargo of youth broke their nails
Bloodied their hands on the gangway's mirage
And gave themselves up without even seeing
The imagined green landscape of the promised land.

III

The young men came in the berths
The young men came in the bunks
The owners of the men came in the cabins
But the cargo which burned in the old morning of the Indian Ocean
Was the cargo of the berths
Was the cargo of the bunks
Was all the merchandise that cried out in vain
In the horror of the grave of salt and burning iron
With the mothers and sisters
The widows and the brothers
The widows and the friends, all travelling
On the left side of the soldiers' khaki uniforms
And their yellow buttons with false golden stars in the night
Of the fatal, bloody route of the slavetraders in the sea.

They came in the berths and the bunks
The sad passengers
Almost soldiers
Almost husbands
Almost widowers and almost men
And almost children too, in their living memories of the hunting
Still hunting lizards
And pressing together like brothers
Against the burning hot vertical walls

Of the tropical zodiac of death freeing them in the holds
And together uniting their last voices
In the last understanding.
And together they spat out the same scorn for the smoke and the
     fire
And gnashed their teeth in the same physical happiness
Clear of the extinct love, burned without connection.

They came in the berths and the bunks
And cotton and young recruits together asked for peace
And they disembarked together on the quays of absolute silence,
Recruits without leather belts girding their kidneys
Mixed in the white gold with ashes and insurance policies
And only with the assurance of the misty eyes of old mothers
Of old fathers and old friends of their recent infancy
And the insurance policy of the misty eyes of their mothers and
     beautiful widows
In the tragic, infinite minutes of longing
In the enigmatic hour of burning sticks of arms and cries
With the beautiful yellow buttons of the shining uniforms,
Single metal flowers blooming in their zenith
Of gunpowder and bursting ammunition
In the common grave of the holds.

IV

They came in the berths
In the sumptuous bunks of the holds,
Beautiful examples of boys nearly men
Who filled the misty eyes of the old mothers
Who dug deeper the wrinkles of the old fathers,
The old friends of twenty years
And the widows and the brothers
The mourning in the newspapers' headlines
And typographically clear photographs on the front pages
Looking at us with the same absorbed stares

Of free adolescents, dead
Who won't grow old any more.

It didn't have a history,
The cargo that burned in the bowels of the monster *Save*,
In the vengeful liquid forests of the sea.
White faces
Dark and brown faces
Curly hair and straight hair
On the same terrible day were in that foundered ship
The same mythic color of the poppies
And the exact total dimension,
The same sated death
In the cargo of insured cotton
And the cargo of young people, uninsured but liberated
From the hellish hold of the burned boat.

Translated by Chris Searle. © 1982 José Craveirinha. Reprinted from *Sunflower of Hope*. By permission of Allison & Busby.
The *Save*, named after a major river whose estuary in southern Mozambique is an
important cotton-growing area, sank off the coast of Mozambique in 1962, at a
time of growing resistance to Portuguese rule. The new recruits for the Portu-
guese Army and the cotton, the two types of cargo carried by the ship, have
symbolic meaning.

Song of the Negro on the Ferry

If you could see me die
The millions of times I have been born . . .

If you could see me weep
The millions of times you have laughed . . .

If you could see me cry out
The millions of times I have kept silent . . .

If you could see me sing
The millions of times I have died
And bled . . .

I tell you, European brother

You would be born
You would weep
You would sing
You would cry out
And you would die
Bleeding . . .
Millions of times like me!!!

Translated from the Portuguese by Philippa Rumsey. © 1967 José Craveirinha.
Reprinted from *African Writing Today*. By permission of the translator.

Mamano

The voice of *mufana*
flooded the city with his accusing sobs
the small ghost
crossed over the night cottoned with mist
and a downtrodden spirit
all his fate thrown out so desperately
in a cry full of his life:
Mamano . . . Mamano . . .

City,
What about the black boy of the streets
lost in the white and evil darkness
(white and evil, a thousand times evil)

the steam whistling through the siren in a frenzy of parting
and the holds filled with the dark, living ores?

What about the black boy, almost naked
barefoot and solitary
in that fatal night of deportation
in which the black anguish crossed the quays
covered the city with its voice
and no one heard it deflowering the silence
of the great houses of armored cement;

City
What about the black boy, almost naked
small ghost, crying in his tongue
Mamano . . . Mamano . . .
in that fatal night that deported
fifty-three women
to the plantations of São Tomé?

Translated from the Portuguese by Chris Searle. © 1982 José Craveirinha. Re-
printed from *Sunflower of Hope*. By permission of Allison & Busby.
Mamano means mummy or mama, a term used in the Maputo area.
Mufana is a kid, or little boy.

GOUVEIA DE LEMOS

Gouveia de Lemos is a Mozambican journalist and poet whose poems have appeared in Portuguese-language reviews and anthologies.

Song of Agony

"Vê nerá, né Verá cufâ?"

I put on a clean shirt
and go to work my contract
    Which of us
    Which of us will come back?
Four and twenty moons
not seeing my women
not seeing my ox
not seeing my land
    Which of us
    Which of us will die?
I put on a clean shirt
and go to work my contract
to work far away.
I go beyond the mountain
into the bush
where the road ends
and the river runs dry.
    Which of us
    Which of us will come back?
    Which of us
    Which of us will die?
Put on a clean shirt
it's time to work the contract.

Get into the wagon, brother
we must travel night and day.
    Which of us
    Which of us will come back?
    Which of us
    Which of us will die?
Which of us will come back
to see women
to see our lands
to see our oxen?
    Which of us will die?
    which of us?
    which of us?

Translated from the Portuguese by Margaret Dickinson. © 1972 Gouveia de
Lemos. Reprinted from *When Bullets Begin to Flower*. By permission of East
African Publishing House Ltd.
"Vê nerá, né Verá cufá?" means "Which of us, which of us will die?"

NOÉMIA DE SOUSA

Noémia de Sousa was born on September 20, 1927, in Maputo, Mozambique. She attended elementary school in Maputo and secondary school in Brazil. From 1951 to 1964 she lived in Lisbon, but later fled into exile in France. She is the first African woman writer to have achieved a reputation as a modern poet, having published in several Brazilian, Portuguese, Angolan, and Mozambican journals and anthologies, sometimes under the pseudonym Vera Micaia.

The Poem of João

João was young like us
João had wide-awake eyes
and alert ears
hands reaching forwards
a mind cast for tomorrow
a mouth to cry an eternal "no"
João was young like us.

João enjoyed art and literature
enjoyed poetry and Jorge Amado
enjoyed books of meat and soul
which breathe life, struggle, sweat and hope
João dreamt of Zambezi's flowing books spreading culture
for mankind, for the young, our brothers
João fought that books might be for all
João loved literature
João was young like us.

João was the father, the mother, the brother of multitudes
João was the blood and the sweat of multitudes
and suffered and was happy like the multitudes

He smiled that same tired smile of shopgirls leaving work
He suffered with the passivity of the peasant women
he felt the sun piercing like a thorn in the Arab's midday
he bargained on bazaar benches with the Chinese
he sold tired green vegetables with the Asian traders
he howled spirituals from Harlem with Marian Anderson
he swayed to the Chope marimbas on a Sunday
he cried out with the rebels their cry of blood
he was happy in the caress of the manioc-white moon
he sang with the *shibalos* their songs of homesick longing
and he hoped with the same intensity of all
for dazzling dawns with open mouths
to sing
João was the blood and sweat of multitudes
João was young like us.

João and Mozambique were intermingled
João would not have been João without Mozambique
João was like a palm tree, a coconut palm
a piece of rock, a Lake Niassa, a mountain
an Incomati, a forest, a maçala tree
a beach, a Maputo, an Indian Ocean
João was an integral and deep-rooted part of Mozambique
João was young like us.

João longed to live and longed to conquer life
that is why he loathed prisons, cages, bars
and loathed the men who make them.
For João was free.
João was an eagle born to fly
João loathed prisons and the men who make them
João was young like us.

And because João was young like us
and had wide-awake eyes
and enjoyed art and poetry and Jorge Amado

and was the blood and sweat of multitudes
and was intermingled with Mozambique
and was an eagle born to fly
and hated prisons and the men who make them
Ah, because of all this we have lost João
We have lost João.

Ah, this is why we have lost João
why we weep night and day for João
for João whom they have stolen from us.

And we ask
But why have they taken João,
João who was young and ardent like us
João who thirsted for life
João who was brother to us all
why have they stolen from us João
who spoke of hope and dawning days
João whose glance was like a brother's hug
João who always had somewhere for one of us to stay

João who was our mother and our father
João who would have been our saviour
João whom we loved and love
João who belongs so surely to us
oh, why have they stolen João from us?
And no one answers
indifferent, no one answers.

But we know
why they took João from us
João, so truly our brother.

But what does it matter?
They think they have stolen him but João is here with us
is here in others who will come

in others who have come.
For João is not alone
João is a multitude
João is the blood and the sweat of multitudes
and João, in being João, is also Joaquim, José
Abdullah, Fang, Mussumbuluco, is Mascarenhas
Omar, Yutang, Fabiao
João is the multitude, the blood and sweat of multitudes.

And who will take José, Joaquim, Abdullah
Fang, Mussumbuluco, Mascarenhas, Omar, Fabiao?
Who?
Who will take us all and lock us in a cage?
Ah, they have stolen João from us
But João is us all
Because of this João hasn't left us
and João "was" not, he "is" and "will be"
For João is us all, we are a multitude
and the multitude
who can take the multitude and lock it in a cage?

Translated from the Portuguese by Margaret Dickinson. © 1972 Noémia de Sousa.
  Reprinted from *When Bullets Begin to Flower*. By permission of East African
  Publishing House Ltd.
The Chope are a people of Inhambane Province and other parts of southern Mo-
  zambique who are master musicians and have been recruited to work in the
  South African mines.

Magaiça

The blue and gold morning of paper propaganda
has engulfed the blockhead, engulfed *mamparra*,
who is utterly dazed
by the meaningless gibber

of the whites on the station
and by the querulous puffing of the trains.
It has swallowed his eyes, round with amazement,
his heart, bound by the pain of the unknown
and his bundle of rags
which is charged with great longings and woven
with *mamparra*'s unrealized dreams.

And one day
the train came back, puffing, puffing,
oh, *nhanisse*, came back.
And with it Magaiça
with overcoat, tie and striped socks,
a being displaced and enmeshed in ridicule.
     —Where has it left you,
that bundle of dreams, Magaiça?
You're carrying cases full of the false glitter
of the remnants of the false culture
of the compound of the Rand.

And, stunned,
Magaiça lit a lamp
to search for lost illusions,
for his youth and his health, which stay buried
deep in the mines of Johannesburg.
Youth and health,
the lost illusions
which will shine like stars
on some Lady's neck in some City's night.

Translated from the Portuguese by Margaret Dickinson. © 1972 by Noémia de
    Sousa. Reprinted from *When Bullets Begin to Flower*. By permission of East
    African Publishing House Ltd.
A *mamparra* is a fool, or a returned migrant worker.
Nhanisse is an exclamation equivalent to "True God" or "Good Lord."

If You Want to Know Me

If you want to know me
examine with careful eyes
this bit of black wood
which some unknown Makonde brother
cut and carved
with his inspired hands
in the distant lands of the North.

This is what I am
empty sockets despairing of possessing life
a mouth torn open in an anguished wound
huge hands outspread
and raised in imprecation and in threat
a body tattooed with wounds seen and unseen
from the harsh whip strokes of slavery
tortured and magnificent
proud and mysterious
Africa from head to foot
this is what I am.

If you want to understand me
come, bend over this soul of Africa
in the black dockworker's groans
the Chopes' frenzied dances
the Changanas' rebellion
in the strange sadness which flows
from an African song, through the night.

And ask no more
to know me
for I'm nothing but a shell of flesh
where Africa's revolt congealed
its cry pregnant with hope.

The Makonde are a northern Mozambican people, famous for their beautiful carvings of mythic figures done in hard black wood, hence its significance for a Negritude poet.

The Changaan (Changana) are a people of the Limpopo River basin and other districts of southern Mozambique.

MARCELINO DOS SANTOS

Marcelino dos Santos, who published under the pseudonyms Kalungano, Micaia, Bébé, and Lilinho during the struggle for independence in Mozambique, was born in 1929 near Lumbo, Mozambique. He was educated at the University of Lisbon and the Sorbonne's Institut des Sciences Politiques and L'Ecole Pratique des Hautes Etudes in Paris, where he remained for ten years. With the formation of FRELIMO (Front for the Liberation of Mozambique), he returned and served as its chief theoretician. His two books of poetry (1959 and 1962), one of which had a preface by Nazim Hikmet, the great Turkish poet, were translated into Russian and published in Moscow. He was the first Vice-President of both FRELIMO and the government of Mozambique, in which he is now Minister of Economic Planning.

Here We Were Born

I

The land where we were born
goes back
like time.

Our forefathers
were born
and lived
in that land

and they, like the coarse wild grass
were the meager body's veins
running red, earth's fragrance.

Trees and granite pinnacles

their arms
embraced the earth
in daily work
and sculpting the new world's fertile rocks
began, in color,
the great design of life.

II

And it was also
here
that you and I were born

hot land
of rising sun

green land
of fertile fields

soft land
with a broad bosom.

It was to us
all this surrendered
brimming with life
and amorous longing.

III

We grew up lulled
by the Chirico's song
and as we reached in this way the level of Man
the impetus was such it generated
waves pregnant with crystal.

And when the wind
whips the sky

and the sword falls
tearing flesh
and horror touches
the naked face

Our love is not shaken.

This is the land
where we were born

its sorrow
is our grief

and today's bitter cloud
is a moment's pain
which the rain must dry.

IV

Our land is open
to the frank embrace of hope.

In the wake of past steps
free orbs come shining

and, as a young brother
of an old land,
let us go
lifting in broad hands
our fathers' heritage
and with the leaves of the heart
carry on man's work
the great design of life.

Translated by Margaret Dickinson. © 1972 Marcelino dos Santos. Reprinted from
When Bullets Begin to Flower. By permission of East African Publishing House
Ltd.

Where I Am

No
Don't look for me
where I don't exist

I live
bent over the earth
following the way written
                    by the whip
on my naked back

I live
in the ports
feeding the furnaces
moving the machines
by the way of men

I live
in my mother's body
selling my flesh
            my sex
            is not for love
I live
lost in the streets
of a civilization
            which crushes me
                        with hatred
                            without pity

And if it's my voice that's heard
and if it's me who still sings
it's because I can't die
            but only the moon listens to my pain

No
don't look for me
in the great halls
       where I'm not
           where I can't be

Here in America
yes
I am also
I am
But Lincoln
was murdered
and I
     I
      I
am lynched every day

The special train
rolling dizzily on the track
is gold
     is blood
which I spilled through the centuries

Why
then
look for me in Beethoven's glory
if I'm here
I am raised up
in the millions of cries
which come from the holds
in all the docksides

and if I'm here
         alive all right
in the voice of Robeson and Hughes
Césaire and Guillén

Godido and Black Boy reborn
in the bowels of the earth
transforming with my body
the foundations of life

if I'm here

the conscious and firm sum
of men
who composed the poem
of life against death
from the end of the night
                    and from the beginning of the day.

The poem "Where I Am" by Kalungano (Marcelino dos Santos) translated by Chris
    Searle, was first published in Searle's anthology *The Sunflower of Hope* (Allison
    & Busky 1982).
Robeson is Paul Robeson, the great Afro-American singer, actor, intellectual, and
    leader.
Hughes is Langston Hughes, Afro-American poet (1902–1967) prominent in the
    Harlem Renaissance of the 1920s.
Césaire is Aimé Césaire, the Martinican poet and leader, internationally famous for
    his long poem *Cahier d'un retour au pays natal* (Return to My Native Land),
    first published by Présence Africaine in Paris in 1956.
Guillén is Nicolas Guillén, the revolutionary poet laureate of Cuba.
Godido is a character in the collection of short stories by Mozambican writer João
    Dias, *Godido e outros contos* (Godido and Other Stories).
Black Boy refers to Richard Wright's *Black Boy*, specifically to the nameless hero.
    This is in keeping with dos Santos's internationalist posture (compare with
    Viriato da Cruz's "Black Mother" vis-à-vis the Black Diaspora).

Dream of the Black Mother

To my Mother

Black mother
Rocks her son
And in her black head

Covered with black hair
She keeps marvelous dreams.

Black mother
Rocks her son
And forgets
That the earth has dried up the maize
That yesterday the groundnuts were finished.

She dreams of marvelous worlds
Where her son would go to school
To school where men study.

Black mother
Rocks her son
And forgets
Her brothers building towns and cities
Cementing them with their blood.

She dreams of marvelous worlds
Where her son would run along the street
The street where men pass by.

Black mother
Rocks her son
And listening
To the voice from afar
Brought by the wind.

She dreams of marvelous worlds
Marvelous worlds
Where her son will be able to live.

Translated from the Portuguese by Philippa Rumsey. © 1967 Marcelino dos Santos.
Reprinted from *African Writing Today*, Es'Kia Mphahlele, ed. By permission of
the translator.

FRELIMO

FRELIMO (Front for the Liberation of Mozambique) was established in Tanzania in 1962 after the merger of several political parties, to fight for the liberation of Mozambique. It is currently the ruling party in Mozambique.

The Guerrilla

There he comes, armed and fierce,
there comes the man who brings freedom;
ragged and dirty, but with an iron heart,
the guerrilla smiles and sings.

He has no home, little food and few clothes,
he lives through suffering.
Torrential rains beat against him,
the bitter cold bites harshly.

Still he smiles and sings.
"I bring peace and freedom;
With this weapon in my hand
I'll drive out Salazar and his troops."

It is a beautiful quiet morning.
The guerrilla awakes.
He has no water.
The dew is his water.

The birds, astonished, ask:
"Why do you suffer, friend?"
The guerrilla smiles and sings:
"I bring freedom for all."

Reprinted from *Mozambique Revolution*. © 1972, 1973, 1974 FRELIMO.

My Brother

My brother
is not he who was born
from the womb of my mother.

My brother
is he who grows with me
in revolt.

He is the one who was born
in the shadows—
the sun was not his,
his land was not his,
his strength was not his,
his wife
was not his.

My brother is the one who does not bend,
does not accept.

He is the one who in the free paths
drinks with me the water of the same river,
sleeps
under the same sky,
sings with me
the same songs of war.

My brother is the one who forgets himself:
the liberation of his people
is his reason for living.

My brother
is that one
at my side
who fights.

Reprinted from *Mozambique Revolution.* © 1972, 1973, 1974 FRELIMO.

Poem Near the Sea

It is not the sea
  casually lapping
    at the white sand

nor
  the moon
    shining smugly
    on the silver fronds of the palm trees.

The essential
    is the new consciousness;
    knowledge
    made instrument of those who do not know.
    Ignorance, superstition, backwardness,
    crumbling like sand castles
    in the wind of science and materialism.

What matters
    is the union of the intellect
    with the hand
    in the collective and liberating act of working the land,
    so that for all will grow
    the undulating green of the maize field.

What matters
    is the mind and the acts and the feeling of each individual
    merging in the community
    like drops of water one by one
    creating an immense ocean that fills the world.

Near the sea,
  a new poem
    for new men.

Reprinted from *Mozambique Revolution.* © 1972, 1973, 1974 FRELIMO.

ARMANDO GUEBUZA

Armando Guebuza was born in 1942 in Mozambique and was educated in Maputo. A FRELIMO (Front for the Liberation of Mozambique) militant, he was once its Inspector of Schools, in charge of primary education in the liberated zones during the armed struggle for independence. He became Minister of the Interior upon independence in 1975 and later served as Vice-Minister of Defense. His poems have appeared in several reviews and anthologies.

Your Pain

Your pain
yet more my pain
shall suffocate oppression

Your eyes
yet more my eyes
shall be speaking of revolt

Your scars
yet more my scars
will be remembering the whip

My hands
yet more your hands
will be lifted fully armed

My strength
yet more your strength
shall overcome imperialism

My blood
yet more your blood
shall irrigate our victory.

If You Ask Me Who I Am

If you ask me
who I am
with that face of yours
seared by marks of evil
and a sinister smile

I'll tell you nothing
I'll tell you nothing

I'll show you the scars of centuries
which furrow my black back
I'll look at you with eyes of hatred
shot red with blood, shed through the years
I'll show you my hut of grass
falling into disrepair
I'll take you to the plantations
where from dawn to dusk
I bend over the soil
as the torturous work
racks my body

I'll take you to the fields full of people
breathing misery every hour

I'll tell you nothing
I'll just show you this

And then
I'll show you the fallen bodies of *my* people
treacherously gunned down,
huts burned,
by *your* people

I'll tell you nothing
but you will know why I fight.

Translated by Margaret Dickinson. © 1972 Armando Guebuza. Reprinted from
   When Bullets Begin to Flower. By permission of East African Publishing House
   Ltd.

JOSINA MACHEL

Josina Machel, who died in 1971 at age twenty-five, was a FRELIMO (Front for the Liberation of Mozambique) militant and the first wife of Samora M. Machel, the President of Mozambique. She distinguished herself as a fearless guerrilla fighter and led many successful ambush operations and offensives against Portuguese positions and installations. An exemplary educationist and a high-quality political cadre, she became a symbol of the new Mozambican woman.

This Is the Time

This is the time we were waiting for.
Our guns are light in our hands,
the reasons and aims of the struggle
clear in our minds.

The blood shed by our heroes
makes us sad but resolute.
It is the price of our freedom.
We keep them close in our hearts.
From their example new generations
—revolutionary generations—
are already being born.

Ahead of us we see bitter hardships.
But we see also
our children running free,
our country plundered no more.

This is the time to be ready
and firm,
the time to give ourselves
to the Revolution.

© 1973 Josina Machel. Reprinted from *Mozambique Revolution*.

SAMORA M. MACHEL

Samora M. Machel, the first President of the People's Republic of Mozambique, distinguished himself in the struggle against Portuguese colonialism. He became the second President of FRELIMO (Front for the Liberation of Mozambique), after the assassination of Dr. Eduardo Mondlane in February 1969. He wrote this poem upon the death of his first wife, Josina, who died during the war, but from natural causes.

Josina, You Are Not Dead

Josina, you are not dead, because we have assumed your responsibilities and they live in us.

You have not died, for the causes you championed were inherited by us in their entirety.

You are gone from us, but the weapon and rucksack that you left, your tools of work, are part of my burden.

The blood you shed is but a small drop in the flood we have already given and still have to give.

The earth must be nourished and the more fertile it is the better do its trees flourish, the bigger are the shadows they cast, the sweeter are their fruits.

Out of your memory I will fashion a hoe to turn the sod enriched by your sacrifice . . . and new fruits will grow.

The Revolution renews itself from its best and most beloved children.

This is the meaning of your sacrifice: it will be a living example to be followed.

My joy is that as patriot and woman you died doubly free
in this time when the new power and the new woman are emerging.

In your last moments you apologized to the doctors for
not being able to help them.

The manner in which you accepted the sacrifice is
an inexhaustible source of inspiration and courage.

When a comrade so completely assumes the new values he wins
our heart, becomes our banner.

Thus more than wife, you were to me sister, friend and comrade-
in-arms.

How can we mourn a comrade but by holding the fallen gun
and continuing the combat.

My tears flow from the same source that gave birth to our love,
our will and our revolutionary life.

These tears are both a token and a vow of combat.

The flowers which fall from the tree are to prepare the land
for new and more beautiful flowers to bloom in the next season.

Your life continues in those who continue the Revolution.

JORGE REBELO

Jorge Rebelo was born in 1940 in Maputo, Mozambique. He was educated at Coimbra University, in Portugal. He served as FRELIMO's (Front for the Liberation of Mozambique) Secretary for Information and Editor of *Mozambique Revolution*, its official organ. He was the first Minister of Information in the new government of Mozambique after independence. His poems have been published in several journals and anthologies. The title of Margaret Dickinson's anthology, *When Bullets Begin to Flower*, is derived from the last two lines of his "Poem": "In our land / Bullets are beginning to flower."

Poem

Come, brother, and tell me your life,
come, show me the marks of revolt
which the enemy left on your body

Come, say to me "Here
my hands have been crushed
because they defended
the land which they own

"Here my body was tortured
because it refused to bend
to invaders

"Here my mouth was wounded
because it dared to sing
my people's freedom"

Come, brother, and tell me your life,
come relate to me the dreams of revolt

which you and your fathers and forefathers
dreamed
in silence
through shadowless nights made for love

Come, tell me these dreams become
war,
the birth of heroes,
land reconquered,
mothers who, fearless,
send their sons to fight

Come, tell me all this, my brother

And later I will forge simple words
which even the children can understand,
words which will enter every house
like the wind
and fall like red-hot embers
on our people's souls

In our land
Bullets are beginning to flower.

Translated by Margaret Dickinson. © 1972 Jorge Rebelo. Reprinted from *When Bullets Begin to Flower*. By permission of East African Publishing House Ltd.

NAMIBIA

> . . . as old
> as all the best wishes in every heart
> (and) as old
> as all the unfulfilled longings
> in every life . . .
> —Mvula Ya Nangolo

NAMIBIA, a former colony of Germany and currently under illegal South African rule, is a country suffering extreme contention. Its poets have adopted English—for them, a third, rather than a second language—as a medium of expression in order to make their case known to a wider audience. Consequently, they face the problems that most third-language users encounter, yet their performance is admirable. Because they suffer from the stranglehold of apartheid, their poetry resembles, even approximates, black South African poetry in its defiant protest against racial bigotry. Simultaneously, their combat poems express their quest for freedom and reconstruction of their communities in a spirit reminiscent of the poetry of Angola and Mozambique, and, to some extent, Zimbabwe.

The themes of apartheid, or racial separation, institutionalized violence and police brutality, black suffering and exploitation, encountered so often in black South African poetry, pervade Namibian poetry as well. Like other poets of the region, Mvula Ya Nangolo and Cosmo Pieterse deal with the persecution, arbitrary imprisonment, police harassment, and the general misery experienced by the black people vis-à-vis the affluence, comfort, hypocrisy, myopia, insensitivity of the white minority population. Yet they are not content with mere exposure of these inequities; they suggest ways in which they may be resolved. And if in their poems they celebrate the armed struggle, it is not because they are inhuman, but because they now recognize their reawakened manhood and their ability actively to transform their societies.

Nangolo's poems show us a world where the black man's lot is one of circumscription: he can no longer gallop like a young zebra or "drink water from ostrich eggs," or hunt, sing, and dance freely. He is dumped in a shack or hut where he "survives like a mouse" ("Contrast"). In a plain, simple, and direct style, characteristic of much of the poetry in this collection, Nangolo tells of the disparities in living standards between whites and blacks. He presents double-image movie stills or slides and a running commentary composed of concrete words—chains, wounds, hardened hands, ceaseless pain, sweat, bleeding heart—to characterize the black man's life. In the adjacent, yet distant, world, the white man's house stands "erect," and he is waited on by aged men and women whom he denies manhood and womanhood, referring to them as "Boy" and "Maid." And the superiority-inferiority dichotomy reaches into the next world, where a black man is buried in a "slaveyard," whereas the white man reposes in a "graveyard." Pieterse, who deals with similar themes in his poems, delivers a pointed sermon ("To White South Africa") in a plain, transparent style and defiant tone similar to those of black South African poetry, accusing the white South Africans of myopia, which prevents them from seeing the hunger, pain, stark misery, and evil they inflict on their black neighbors.

There is no hermetic narcissism or poetic posturing here; the simple word and the basic syntactic structure are adequate vehicles for the message or the threat, as in Nangolo's "Guerrilla Promise." "I'll rush upon you / like escaping new-born sun ray," the guerrilla says, and, boasting of his prowess, he identifies himself with his weaponry: "I'm a poisoned arrow // I'm strong-bow / I'm a sharpened spear / I'm a sword." Yet the guerrilla is not a bloodhound; he is warm and humane, as "The Guerrilla" by FRELIMO demonstrates. Indeed, in another Nangolo poem ("A Flower"), the voice of a dead freedom fighter exhorts the poet to "put a flower on my grave / for I died like a brave." In many of these poems, one hears resonances of African ritual chants, as in Pieterse's "Song (We Sing)," written in the incantatory style of Angolan and Mozambican combat poetry. He uses the oral poetic device of repetition innovatively, by distributing the phrase "We sing" throughout the poem, perhaps to create an impression of spontaneity in the celebration of the death of young guerrillas. The poet, assuming a communal voice, welcomes this death as necessary in the land's cycle of growth and renewal. The life thus given is the "seed of the land" that yields "flowers / Of manhood, of labor, of spring." In "Guerrilla," Pieterse addresses his "Mother, stepmotherland" (for he was born in Windhoek, Namibia, but of South African parents) in affectionate tones, demonstrating the fighter's ability to modulate his voice from extreme anger to tenderness. This intimate attachment to land as mother or lover is one of the thematic threads that run through the poetry of Angola (especially that of Agostinho Neto), Mozambique (in Marcelino dos Santos), Malawi, Botswana, Zimbabwe, and South Africa.

MVULA YA NANGOLO

Mvula Ya Nangolo was born on August 9, 1943, in Oniimwandi Village, Uukwambi District, in northern Namibia. He is an accomplished journalist who has worked for two major radio networks in Central Europe. He also helped launch "The Namibian Hour" on Radio Tanzania, in Dar es Salaam, and has worked as commentator, producer, and news reader for Radio Zambia in Lusaka. He has published feature articles in the *Daily News* and *Sunday News*, Tanzania, *Times of Zambia* and *Sunday Times*, Zambia, *Namibia–Today* (SWAPO), and *Africa Magazine*, London. He works for the Department of Information and Publicity and edits *Namibia–Today*, the official organ of the South West African People's Organization (SWAPO). His privately printed chapbook, *From Exile*, is the only book of poems in English by a Namibian writer.

Hunter's Song

I

When time was then
  my people then
began to sing or dance
  to the most beautiful tune of Mama nature
nothing scarce but food in abundance
  they sang songs in praise of the rising sun
adored the new moon but soon thought
  how wonderful a world
how beautiful a people they were
  this, when time was then.

II

Now that Mama nature is as old
  as all the best wishes in every heart

now that she's as old
   as all the unfulfilled longings
in every life
   the hunter's song is loud and clear
his heart beats far slower
   he's swiftly approaching the noon of his life

III

Son of my *khoi-khoi*
   you can no longer gallop like a young zebra
you can no longer drink water from ostrich eggs
   in faraway places
they've taken your bow
   and you've nothing to show
they've hidden your poisoned arrow
   till tomorrow
thus, Kalahari, brave of my roaming *khoi-khoi* clan
   wait till tomorrow
and away with sorrow.

IV

When death comes prowling like a leopard
   you said you'll know it's time to depart
but for the time being
   you wish to see those bare sand dunes of the
   Namib
you wish not to inhale polluted air
   you wish for the cooling shade of the great
Baobab
   where many moons ago you were born
and now that it's the norm
   to rest buried in a numbered grave
what do you think of every morn of your life?
   hunters', hunters' son—my *khoi-khoi* brave?

V

Let us together now
 before your eyes are closed
and your heart stops dancing to the tune of life
 let us together now

do the frog dance before tomorrow
 praise our ancestors without sorrow
and then search where they'd hidden your bow
 I need your poisoned arrow tomorrow.

Khoi-khoi means "people's people" in the Nama language of Namibia, from *khoi* meaning "person," "human being," or "people."

Contrast

I

Across the hill stands erect a white man's house;
 in a poorly ventilated shack the black man
survives like a mouse,

a shadowy body in motion coupled with a human
 heart in confinement:
chains at heart—the wound of suffering oozing
 ceaseless pain,

sweat drops zigzagging down his muscled black
 neck in vain;
handkerchief not possessed, the hardened black
 hand wipes it off,
bleeding heart and the vein of reason punctured
 irreparably.

II

Across the hill stands erect a white man's house,
   a mile or two away a black worker's hut.
Much the white man sips his wine—an alcoholic;
   much the black man drinks his brew—a drunkard.
Equal?
   Not even when they are dead:
There . . . a white man's graveyard,
   here . . . a black man's slaveyard.

III

My aging Papa is called a Boy;
   white man insists on being called Mr. Man.
My Mama, my Papa's wife, is called a Maid;
   white woman insists on being called Mrs.
   Somebody.

I am called a black thieving brat;
   my (white) agemate, a beautiful child of
Mr. and Mrs. So-and-So.

IV

Across the hill stands erect a white man's house;
   black man's shack is empty,
   he's gone with his spouse

   to join fighters
   forever opposed
   contrast imposed
   by those who supposed
   black man is less human
   but who then is a louse?

Guerrilla Promise

I'll rush upon you
    like escaping newborn sunray
then dazzle you with my lethal swiftness
    'cause I'm the Fight

As unknown as an unborn battle
    laboring with steel and hand grenade
I'm death conceived

    till my moment arrives
with pain . . . blood and terror
    I'm a soldier of this realm
I'm a poisoned arrow

    I'm a string-bow
I'm a sharpened spear
    I'm a sword

waiting in my sheath
    only for your death.

A Flower

Ever walked that footpath
    to my village
between that communal well
    and your uncle's homestead?
If next you come
    not by flying machine

but walking in single file
　　with your chum and scum
from the city . . .
　　just don't walk by
but stop

Put a flower on my grave
　　for I died like a brave
for your salary so high
　　which you receive with no sigh
I'd freed you
　　and lest you forget the brave

there on my grave
　　just a flower—child
onto my eternal bed
　　where I rest but not yet dead
just a flower lad.

1975

COSMO PIETERSE

Cosmo Pieterse was born in 1930 in Windhoek, Namibia, of South African parents. He was educated at the University of Cape Town, where he obtained a B.Ed. and an M.A. in English and Nederlands en Afrikaans. For eleven years he taught in a Cape Town school. In 1962 he was banned under the Riotous Assemblies Act, and in 1965 left the country on an exit visa. He has been an actor, lecturer, broadcaster, and teacher in London. He taught for six years at Ohio University, and is now teaching English in Bulawayo, Zimbabwe. He has edited and co-edited six anthologies of African plays, essays, and interviews with African writers, among them: *Ten One Act Plays; Protest and Conflict in African Literature; African Writers Talking; Seven South African Poets*, and *Speak Easy, Speak Free*. He has published two volumes of his own poetry and contributed to many publications.

To White South Africa

If, when you walk around the Cape's sand flats,
You do not see men laugh or sing or play,
But only hear them swear and shout, then say
That here are those who work in your stone flats;
Who walk your streets; who see your sights; who are
Your blood, your sin, your guilt, your crime; who own
No color in their lives but their own;
Who live with it in the dark because you bar
From light the children of the sun, who pray
To God for help that never came or will;
Who are to hunger, pain, each human ill,
Just as you are, and last to death, all prey . . .
Your wealth feeds want, two thousand miles o'ersea—
You're blind to, ten miles from your eyes, stark misery.

Song (We Sing)

We sing our sons who have died red
Crossing the sky where barbed wire passes
Bullets of white paper, nails of grey lead
And we sing the moon in its dying phases.

We sing the moon, nine blue moons of being
We sing the moons of barren blood
Blood of our daughters, waters fleeing
From bodiless eyes that have stared and dried.

The seed of the land we sing, the flowers
Of manhood, of labor, of spring
We sing the deaths we welcome as ours
And the birth from the dust that is green we sing.

Guerrilla

I sometimes feel a cold love burning
Along the shuddering length of all my spine;
It's when I think of you with some kind of yearning,
Mother, stepmotherland, who drop your litter with a bitter
    spurning.

And then I know, quite quietly and sure, just how
Before the land will take new seed, even before we forge a single
    plough,
We'll have to feel one sharp emotion deep, resolve one deed:

That we must march over the length of all your life, transgressing
    your whole body with harsh boots upon our feet.
But even then there must also remain somewhere within your
    tissued depth
    Some little corners of an undisguised
        motherliness to bleed
Warmth in which we may dream sleep, where we might
        cling and find remission, help;
    on which our deeds may feed their hunger unsurprised,
        to which our suffering needs
    even and all our death must lead.

SOUTH AFRICA

I do not know where I have been,
But, Brother,
I know I'm coming:
I come like a tide of water now.

       —Mongane Wally Serote

The sound begin again:
the siren in the night
the thunder at the door
the shriek of nerves in pain.

       —Dennis Brutus

THIS SECTION, the largest in this anthology, contains poems on a wider variety and range of themes, styles, and tonal frequencies than the rest of the collection. Black Africans constitute not only a majority, but also the largest group of English-language users in South Africa, where English is fast becoming an African language, especially with the growth of the Black Consciousness movement in ghettos such as Soweto. A considerable body of English-language poetry continues to flourish in the urban centers and racially segregated areas.

Although the poets here range from "colored" to black, according to racial classification under apartheid, they share common experiences under the oppressive regime. Their poems deal with the plight of people in the slums, and thematically they are similar to Angolan and Mozambican protest poetry as well as to Namibian and Zimbabwean poetry. Apartheid is a major theme, and it is related to the recurrent themes of institutionalized violence, detention, deprivation and dispossession, dehumanization, despair and suffering, squalor and starvation in the slums, Black Conscousness, which echoes the Negritude theme in Angolan and Mozambican poetry, kinship, love, and hope.

There is a noticeable quest for, and tendency toward, a simple and direct style in the work of Dennis Brutus, Mbuyiseni Oswald Mtshali, Sipho Sepamla, and Mongane Wally Serote, who reject ornate style and embellishment in favor of a clearly articulated message, strengthened by vivid imagery. The poetry has sparse, yet stark, evocative imagery, which delineates immediate experience and scene as graphically as some of the poems from Angola, Mozambique, and Zimbabwe. Much of it has the oral quality that marks the poetry of the region, an African characteristic created by the use of repetitive refrains and lines or verses from work songs and chants, often encountered in the poems of Agostinho Neto, Antonio Jacinto, and other poets of Angola, as well as Marcelino dos Santos, José Craveirinha, and Noémia de Sousa of Mozambique. There is a strong improvisational element in some of the poems, especially in Keorapetse Kgositsile's and Serote's, which pulsate with forceful, thrusting, vigorous, at times jumpy and fast-paced rhythm from traditional African song, spirituals, and other oral forms. Many of the poets experiment with language, using both colloquial and standard English, drawing on the vocabulary and syntax of the townships.

There are two exceptional poets here whose work may appear different from the rest of the poetry in this collection. Arthur Nortje, who died at twenty-seven, wrote some very difficult poems, using a complex style. Intensely personal, they are characterized by incredible nervous energy, cerebral imagery, and introspection. The other poet, Mazisi Kunene, deliberately writes in the Zulu literary tradition; his poetry owes its style and language, its characteristically communal and oral quality, to Zulu oral poetic forms, such as the heroic epic and the praise poem. His poems are strongly eloquent, oratorical and rhetorical, dramatic, with strong internal rhythms, concrete imagery, and traditional symbolism.

Although these are protest poems, their tones range from somber and quiet anger to the strident, passionate, and defiantly aggressive tones of Namibian, Angolan, and Mozambican poetry. Irony and wit are favored, perhaps because of the strict censorship laws, which are applied mainly to black African writing. Most of the major poets have had some or all of their work banned from circulation in South Africa.

South Africa continues to be one of the worst police states in the world today; its black population remains disenfranchised, and lives under uncertainties, manifold restrictions, constant evictions, and circumscription. As a result, many black people are physically so rootless that they can no longer recognize their ancestral lands. Under these worsening conditions, it is to be expected that the themes of oppression, hate, despair, suffering, institutionalized violence, death, and the insensitivity of white authorities to such pain and suffering will continue to pervade black South African poetry, which, in its protest, is bound to assume angrier and more defiant and passionate tones. Poetry will become more functional, will be a weapon in the armed struggle that has already started.

DENNIS BRUTUS

Dennis Brutus is the best known of the South African poets. He was born in Harare, Zimbabwe, but grew up in Dowerville township, Port Elizabeth, South Africa. After graduating in arts from Fort Hare University College, he taught English and Afrikaans in high school for fourteen years, until he was dismissed in 1962 for his antiapartheid activities. He studied law at the University of Witwatersrand, in Johannesburg, where he was active in the struggle against racism in South African sports. He was arrested, banned, shot in the stomach in an attempt to leave South Africa, and imprisoned, for eighteen months' hard labor, on Robben Island. Released in 1965, but unable to publish or even write because of further banning orders, he left the country in 1966 on an exit permit. After settling briefly in England, he traveled to the United States, where he has taught at the University of Denver and is now teaching at Northwestern University. Among his books of poetry are *Sirens, Knuckles, Boots, Letter to Martha and Other Poems from a South African Prison, Poems from Algiers, A Simple Lust, Strains, China Poems*, and *Stubborn Hope*. His latest volume of poetry, *Censures and Salutes*, is to be published by Fourth Dimension Publishers, in Nigeria.

On the Island

I

Cement-grey floors and walls
cement-grey days
cement-grey time
and a grey susurration
as of seas breaking
winds blowing
and rains drizzling

A barred existence
so that one did not need to look
at doors or windows
to know that they were sundered by bars
and one locked in a grey gelid stream
of unmoving time.

2

When the rain came
it came in a quick moving squall
moving across the island
murmuring from afar
then drumming on the roof
then marching fading away.

And sometimes one mistook
the weary tramp of feet
as the men came shuffling from the quarry
white-dust-filmed and shambling
for the rain
that came and drummed and marched away.

3

It was not quite envy
nor impatience
nor irritation
but a mixture of feelings
one felt
for the aloof deep-green dreaming firs
that poised in the island air
withdrawn, composed and still.

4

On Saturday afternoons we were embalmed in time
like specimen moths pressed under glass;

we were immobile in the sunlit afternoon
waiting;
visiting time:
until suddenly like a book snapped shut
all possibilities vanished as zero hour passed
and we knew another week would have to pass.

The "Island" refers to Robben Island Prison, off Cape Town, where Brutus was imprisoned for eighteen months.

The Sounds Begin Again

The sounds begin again:
the siren in the night
the thunder at the door
the shriek of nerves in pain.

Then the keening crescendo
of faces split by pain,
the wordless, endless wail
only the unfree know.

Importunate as rain
the wraiths exhale their woe
over the sirens, knuckles, boots;
my sounds begin again.

Letter #18

I remember rising one night
after midnight
and moving
through an impulse of loneliness
to try and find the stars.

And through the haze
the battens of fluorescents made
I saw pinpricks of white
I thought were stars.

Greatly daring
I thrust my arm through the bars
and easing the switch in the corridor
plunged my cell in darkness

I scampered to the window
and saw the splashes of light
where the stars flowered.

But through my delight
thudded the anxious boots
and a warning barked
from the machine-gun post
on the catwalk.

And it is the brusque inquiry
and threat
that I remember of that night
rather than the stars.

20 December 1965

Somehow We Survive

Somehow we survive
and tenderness, frustrated, does not wither.

Investigating searchlights rake
our naked unprotected contours;

over our heads the monolithic decalogue
of fascist prohibition glowers
and teeters for a catastrophic fall;

boots club on the peeling door.

But somehow we survive
severance, deprivation, loss.

Patrols uncoil along the asphalt dark
hissing their menace to our lives;

most cruel, all our land is scarred with terror,
rendered unlovely and unlovable;
sundered are we and all our passionate surrender

but somehow tenderness survives.

Blood River Day

for Daphne Edmondson

Each year on this day
they drum the earth with their boots
and growl incantations
to evoke the smell of blood
for which they hungrily sniff the air:

guilt
drives them to the lair
of primitiveness
and ferocity:

but in the dusk
it is the all pervasive smell of dust
the good smell of the earth
as the rain sifts down on the hot sand
that comes to me

the good smell of the dust
that is the same
everywhere around the earth.

December 16, 1965

The Beauty of My Land Peers Warily

The beauty of my land peers warily
through palisading trees on hilly slopes;
at night along the tree-fenced roads
I sense her presence pacing sinuously
beyond the searching circle of the lights.
Exploring pools of soothing tepidness
I find the indrawn nerveless diffidence
of beauty fearing ravishment's delight;
I shiver at her self-defensive scorn
in chillness of aloofly soaring rocks—
But all of these my unwearying ardor mocks
when sunfire ignites the miles of rippling corn.

MAFIKA PASCAL GWALA

Mafika Pascal Gwala, son of a "colored" mother and an African father, was born in 1946 in Verulam, South Africa. He attended Catholic mission schools and Inkamana High School, Vryheid, and entered Ngoye University, but later dropped out. He became a leading exponent of Black Consciousness, and wrote three position papers for the South African Students Organisation (SASO) General Students Council in 1972, 1974, and 1976. In 1977 he was detained for one hundred days during the regime's campaign against Black Consciousness organizations. He has worked as a legal clerk, secondary-school teacher, factory worker, personnel officer, and publications researcher. He edited *Black Review 1973*; his articles and poems have appeared in journals and anthologies in South Africa; he has published two books of poetry: *Jol'iinkomo* and *No More Lullabies*. He teaches in Hammarsdale.

Sunset

Like icing on a cake,
circles of silvery clouds
frill the setting sun;
inviting a cool evening air,
to soothe the valley
below the Insikeni hills.
A freight train
rumbles down the slope
in geometric fashion;
into the Malenge Valley.
Willowy women
in German Colonial dresses,
joke it up from the water hole;
with ad-bright five-gallon drums
on their black doeks.

Clusters of rondavels
like the brown poisonous mushrooms
that the people do not feed on,
gargling ghetto commotions,
spreading them in torrential drops,
not across; the hopscotch rhythm of
these crowded huts can be the
right thing too.
Mbothwe's Ford tractor
hollers for breath;
under a pressing load of wood
the driver armed with a balaclava
against the wind.
A *baasboy* perches on a cross-pole,
counts the stock of horses
arrested for stray grazing.
A primitive sledge
drawn by cows and oxen
grades out stones
on the tawny road.
A meat hawker
begs us to buy the last two pieces
of meat he wants to part with, fast;
"Just to empty the basket."
As we claw up the path
above the valley
rays of the sun
hustle to filter into the clouds;
descending the eastern horizon,
fragments of cloudlets break
into light rain.

From the Outside

We buried Madaza
on a Sunday;
big crowd:
hangarounds, churchgoers,
drunks and goofs;
even the fuzz
were there
as the priest
hurried
the burial sermon—
and we filled the grave
with red soil,
the mourning song
pitched fistedly high;
what got my brow itching though
is that none
of the cops present
dared to stand out
and say
Madaza was a "Wanted."

Promise!

"At least we can meet at the Indian Market,"
she said way back in Cato Manor.
Haven't met her since.
She, pushed into Umlazi;
Me, pushed into Kwa-Mashu.
She looks at the city from the south;

I descend upon it from the north.
Looks like we've been both lost in the grey
dizziness of our townships. That we can't meet.
OR—who hasn't kept the promise?

The Shebeen Queen

She stood at the factory gate
as she watched
her last debtor approach,
vooping his oversized overalls.
Her last Friday's collection
at this firm. Fifteen of them all
"Come boetie shine up."
The man pulled out the bank notes
—with a quivering smile.
"Gosh, more than half his wages;
I didn't force it
                on him."
She zipped her fat purse and
they walked across the crowded street
into a butchery.
When they whisked out
he had, tucked under his arm,
a plastic bag: fowl heads and feet.
And she—exposed out
of her tight shopper: a broiler.

Shebeen (from the Irish) is an unlicensed drinking house significant at a time
    when South African law prohibited hard liquor for Africans. A shebeen queen
    is a woman of the townships who ran a shebeen and traded in contraband liquor.

KEORAPETSE KGOSITSILE

Keorapetse Kgositsile was born in 1938 in Johannesburg, South Africa. He fled from apartheid in the early sixties, worked for *Spearhead* Magazine in Dar es Salaam, and studied at various American universities, including Columbia, from which he received an M.F.A. in creative writing. He returned to teach English at the University of Dar es Salaam, and he is now teaching at Nairobi University. Among his books are *My Name Is Afrika, For Melba, Spirits Unchained, The Present Is a Dangerous Place, Places and Bloodstains,* and *Heartprints.* He has edited an anthology of African poetry, *The Word Is Here.* His poems have been published in numerous journals and anthologies.

New Age

The questions which have always been here
Jump at us like impatient lovers
Of nights which cannot be numbed
Not even by spirits departed by bottle or land

When fogs of despair jump up thick in our heads
When struggle becomes the next bottle
Or the warmth between a willing woman's thighs
Sucking into her our hasty greed
Remember O comrade commander of the ready smile
This is pain and decay of purpose

Remember in baton boot and bullet ritual
The bloodhounds of Monster Vorster wrote
SOWETO over the belly of my land
With the indelible blood of infants
So the young are no longer young
Not that they demand a hasty death

The past is also turbulent
Ask any traveler with memory
To tame it today is our mission
With liberty hammered to steel in our eye

Remember O Poet
When some of your colleagues meet
They do not talk the glories of the past
Or turn their tongues backwards
In platitudes or idealistic delirium
About change through chance or beauty
Or the perversion you call love
Which be nothing nothing
But the Western pairing of parasites

The young whose eyes carry neither youth nor cowardice
The workers whose song of peace
Now digs graves for the gold-fanged monsters
With artistic precision and purpose
Now know the past is turbulent
We must tame it now
Ask any eye fuelled with liberty

Tell those with ears to hear tell them
Tell them my people are a garden
Rising out of the rancid rituals of rape and ruin
Tell them tell them in the dry season
Leaves will dry and fall to fertilize the land
Whose new flowers black green and gold
Are a worker's song of fidelity
To the land that mothered you

SOWETO ("South West Townships") is a star-shaped matchbox housing complex
  for African workers outside Johannesburg. It was the scene of a massacre of
  African schoolchildren by South African police in June 1976.

Requiem for My Mother

As for me
The roads to you
Lead from any place
Woman dancer-of-steel
Mother daughter sister
Of my young years
The roads to you
Lead from any place
I am.

I do not know
If you hollered in delirium
Like an incontinent dotard
I do not know if you gasped
For the next breath, gagging
Fighting to hold your life in
I do not know if you took
Your last breath with slow resignation
But this I know

I dare not look myself
In the eye peeled red
With despair and impotent regret
I dare not look myself
In the ear groaning
Under these years and tears
I dare not mourn your death
Until I can say without
The art of eloquence
Today we move we move

As for me I will
Never again see the slow
Sadness of your eye
Though it remains

Fixed and talks
Through a grave I do not know
I teeter through
The streets of our anguish
Through this incontinent time and referent
And when I try to Scream *Vengeance*
My voice limps under the cacophony
Of them whose tongue is glued
To the bloodstains in the imperial
Monster's hallways and appetite

As for me
The roads to you
Lead from any place
Though I will never again
Know the morning odor
Of your anxious breath!
Don't let the sun shine
In your arse my child
We do not do those things
Though I will never again
Know your armpit odor
Before the ready-for-work mask
Though I will never again
See the slow sadness of your smile
Under the sun
Woman mother daughter sister
The slow sadness in your eye
Remains fixed and talks
Even here where the amber bandages
Of the sun kiss the day
Before they disappear beyond
These white-hooded mountains and appetites

MAZISI KUNENE

Mazisi Kunene was born in 1930 in Durban, South Africa, where he received an M.A. In 1959 he went to London to work on a thesis on Zulu poetry at the London School of Oriental and African Studies. His book *Zulu Poems* was published there, as was his 400-page *Emperor Shaka the Great.* He has contributed poems to numerous journals and anthologies, and has lectured widely in Europe and the United States. He is teaching at the University of California, Los Angeles.

Thought on June 26

Was I wrong when I thought
All shall be avenged?
Was I wrong when I thought
The rope of iron holding the neck of young bulls
Shall be avenged?
Was I wrong
When I thought the orphans of sulphur
Shall rise from the ocean?
Was I depraved when I thought there need not be love,
There need not be forgiveness, there need not be progress,
There need not be goodness on the earth,
There need not be towns of skeletons,
Sending messages of elephants to the moon?
Was I wrong to laugh asphyxiated ecstasy
When the sea rose like quicklime
When the ashes were blown by the wind
When the infant sword was left alone on the hilltop?
Was I wrong to erect monuments of blood?
Was I wrong to avenge the pillage of Caesar?
Was I wrong? Was I wrong?

Was I wrong to ignite the earth
And dance above the stars
Watching Europe burn with its civilization of fire,
Watching America disintegrate with its gods of steel,
Watching the persecutors of mankind turn into dust
Was I wrong? Was I wrong?

June 26, 1912, is the founding date of the African National Congress of South
   Africa.

To Africa

A salute to the first earth
A salute to the first children
Who found a continent and strange sounds.
A salute to the breath of the wise birds
Who inhabit the echoings of a variegated paradise.
Before us in the beginning of time
In the blue infinite of a million centuries
When the round cloud of gold shrouded the sun
There was the eagle
There was the woman holding the fertile soil
There was the man dreaming the mountains
The seed of the egg was the beginning.
Mother of continents, begetter of children
Giver of plentifulness
Supporter of the mountains with milk
See how their shadows have followed the night
See how they stand beyond the season of our feet
We who inherit the eye and the heart of the leopard.

Bring us the triumphal song
Bring us the sacred sword!

The Political Prisoner

I desired to talk
And talk with words as numerous as sands,
The other side of the wire,
The other side of the fortress of stone.

I found a widow traveling,
Passing the prisoners with firewood.
It is this woman who forbade me to sleep,
Who filled me with dreams.

The dream is always the same.
It turns on an anchor
Until it finds a place to rest:
It builds its cobwebs from the hours.

One day someone arrives and opens the gate.
The sun explodes its fire,
Spreading its flame over the earth,
Touching the spring of mankind.

Behind us there are mountains
Where the widow is abandoned.
She remains there unable to give birth,
Priding herself only in the shadows of yesterdays.

Vengeance

How would it be if I came in the night
And planted the spear in your side
Avenging the dead:
Those you have not known,
Those whose scars are hidden,
Those about whom there is no memorial,
Those you only remembered in your celebration?
We did not forget them.
Day after day we kindled the fire,
Spreading the flame of our anger
Round your cities,
Round your children,
Who will remain the ash-monuments
Witnessing the explosions of our revenge.

ZINDZI MANDELA

Zindzi Mandela is the daughter of Nelson Mandela, the President of the African National Congress of South Africa, who has been imprisoned since 1962, and Winnie Mandela, who has also spent prolonged periods in detention and is now under house arrest in a remote part of South Africa. She has published two collections of her poems: *Black as I Am* and *Black and Fourteen*.

There's an Unknown River in Soweto

There's an unknown river in Soweto
some say it flows with blood
others say it flows with tears
a leader says
it flows with health and purity
the kind of water
that nobody drinks in Soweto

There's an unknown tree in Soweto
some say it bears sorrow
others say it bears death
a leader says
it bears health and purity
the kind of fruit
that nobody tastes in Soweto

There's an unknown river in Soweto
there's an unknown tree in Soweto
the body
the blood
both unknown

I Saw as a Child

I saw as a child
a small white boy
sitting in a car

and I never knew why
when my home was so far
and his so near
I had to walk
I saw as a child
a tall building
beautiful and empty
and I never knew why
when my home was so small
and this so big
we were overcrowded

I saw as a child
a tarred road
clean and lonely

and I never knew why
when our street was so busy
and this so alone
it was uncared for

Echo of Mandela

In silence
the distant heroes bow their
heads
the chains weigh them down
they know no laughter
retreating . . . retreating
into a mist of bloodiness
the decaying skull
of buried freedom
emits a dull echo
of cries
free me
free me
the people are calling
looking back
they see nothing but death
where is the welcome
why the sound of tears
hammering . . . hammering
those coffins of confessions
the decaying skull
of buried freedom
emits a dull echo
of cries
free me
free me
the people are calling
tomorrow has come
the distant heroes stand above
they look down
they shake their heads
whispering . . . whispering
into ears of emptiness
the decaying skull

of buried freedom
emits a dull echo
of cries
free me
free me
the people are calling
South Africa, are you listening?

Mandela refers to Nelson Mandela, her father, the leader of the African National
Congress, imprisoned for twenty years (1962–1982) on Robben Island, then
secretly transferred to Pollsmoor Prison on the mainland, about twenty kilome-
ters from Cape Town, in April 1982.

Drink from My Empty Cup

Drink from my empty cup
and be proud
that nothing could quench your thirst

the reality
satisfied you
likewise
be hungry
crave for food
tremble at the sight of beer

kill
and feel free
then know
that you are so oppressed
you even laugh at yourself

DON MATTERA

Don Mattera was born in 1935 in Johannesburg's Western Native Township, South Africa. He is a journalist and poet. Banned while working on the newspaper *Star* in Johannesburg, he was unbanned in the early eighties. Some of his poems have appeared in *African Arts* and *Index on Censorship*, but most of them remain in manuscript form, as "Poems from Shackles," as does an autobiography, "Gone with the Twilight." He lives in Soweto, South Africa.

Protea

The Protea is not a flower
    It is a dome of fluttering flags
    tombs of Afrikaner relics
    and monuments of ox wagon
    dipped in blood

It is the flight of the Blackman's spear
    flung in hostile fear
    of lost possession
    Conquered manhood and broken pride

It is tears
    of my bonded people
    falling on Pretoria's marble steps
    the victims of subjugation

The Protea can never be a flower
    Not while the soul
    of South Africa struggles to be set free. . . .

Of Reason and Discovery

I have dispensed with reasoning
It blinded me to many wrongs
nearly robbed me of sanity
I once reasoned with the whiteman's evil
saw his crimes against my people
his weakness and human folly
God would right the wrong, they said
But they did not say when
So, I have dispensed with reasoning
for it clouds a Blackman's vision
blunts his wrath and makes him tolerant
of his oppression
        I have discovered, yes
the reason for all this hurt
this long deep searching
of scanning the Godless sky
for the suspended reply
        I have discovered, yes
the fault not in the God
nor the pain, but the sufferer
who makes virtue of his anguish
and waits meekly on the God
for deliverance
though white scavengers rip flesh
from his battered black bones
        I have discovered, yes
the yoke is comfortable
when the belly is full
and there is time to pray for peace
though police guns rattle on mine dunes
in the name of protection and order
        I have discovered, yes
that an ounce of gold
exceeds the value of a Blackman's life

and there is no more time to reason and pray
                    Yes, I have discovered yes . . .

At Least

This day at least
let me see the hours through
without a wince
of discontent
as I drop
the heavy cloak
of bitter resolve
to welcome the infiltration
of warmth and love and beauty

This day at least
let me be moved away
from the ghosts
of pained exhortation
that lacerate the heart
embittered emotion

For these brief
somewhat fleeting hours
while the crisp laughter
of the wind fills me deeply
O my land,
at least for this untroubled day
let me unclench my being
to stroke the yellow flowers

BONISILE JOSHUA MOTAUNG

Bonisile Joshua Motaung is a South African poet and a member of the Bayajula Artists group in Kwa Thema Township. His poems have appeared in *Staffrider* magazine, which is published in Johannesburg.

The Garden Boy

He lived amid the floricultural attractions
Of the white suburbs.
He's unknown to his people and the state,
Known to his employer and to his duty.
He never schooled, but he can english.
He knows Verwoerd and has seen King George
And never forgets to say,
"How good they were."

He is the only black rose among
The white daisies and lilies.
The lawns he tends are greener
Than the grass he smokes.
"Keep off the grass," he shouts
Whenever his brother comes for garbage.
He lives to see the happiness of others
Which is of his making:
The florist wears his dignity
And pockets his emoluments.

His possessiveness knows no law,
Color or creed.
They are all his,
My *baas*, my missis

My *baas se vrou*, my *vrou se baas*.
He sings the music of the birds,
Listens to the humming bees
And dances spade in hand as the flowers
Sway from side to side.

He prefers to be called
Jim, Dick, John or Petros
Rather than Boy.
And whenever the missis shouts "Boy!" . . .
He never responds,
But says "SHIT!" . . .
Without being heard.

EZEKIEL MPHAHLELE

Ezekiel Mphahlele, born in 1919 in Pretoria, South Africa, is a well-known writer, scholar, and teacher. He has written three volumes of short stories: *Man Must Live and Other Stories, The Living and the Dead, and Other Stories,* and *In Corner B*; an autobiography: *Down Second Avenue*; two novels: *The Wanderers* and *Chirundu*; two books of literary criticism: *The African Image* and *Voices in the Whirlwind and Other Essays.* He earned a Ph.D. in creative writing at the University of Denver and has taught in many universities in Africa, the United States, and South Africa. After many years in exile, he returned, a few years ago, to teach and live in South Africa.

A Poem

For all the victims of racist tyranny in southern Africa

What is there that we can do or say
will sustain them
in those islands
where the sun was made for janitors?

What is there that we can say or do
will tear the years
from out the hands
of savages who man the island galleys,

will bring them home and dry and mend them
bring them back
to celebrate
with us the song and dance and toil of living?

What is it that we can do or say
will send the plague

among the bandits
that watch and wait to wreck the freedom train?

The hounds are breeding where our house is fallen
ourselves we roam
the wilderness
"Go tell them there across the seas go tell him

tell them that his mother's dead six years
hounds are watching
hounds are waiting—
she told him not to write no more no more."

You who fell before the cannon or
the sabered tooth
or lie on hallowed
ground: O tell us what to say or do.

So many routes have led to exile since
your day, our Elders,
we've been here
and back in many cycles oh so many

Cheap and easy answers have been chewed up
ready to
pop like bubble gum
for exile is   a ghetto of the mind:

new terrain different drummers borrowed
dreams, and there
behind us now
the hounds have diamond fangs and paws of steel.

Perhaps we still can sing *a better day's*
a-coming soon

so *we* don't break:
in our deflated days we want a center.

No time for dirge or burial without corpses:
teach us, Elders,
how to wait
and feel the center, tame the time like masters.

Suspended self like fireflies must come
to earthy center,
sing the blues
so pain will bleed and let the islands in.

Homeward Bound

The mountains that I like
and do not fear
don't stoop over me
like giant apes marooned
on a patch of Time;

they are the forms beyond,
holding down
the edge of blue
and etching with a light
of ever-changing tints;

—they can look the way I want them.

I do not like the lights
that come at me
and stab and flail
and blind the eyes of night
that bounce and cling on tarmac;

those shimmering faraway bodies
softly throbbing
tell me and love
that coffee's on the boil,
she's listening for my footsteps;

—they can look the way I want them.

But you beside me here—
the contours of
your mountainscape
lead me to sniff at the corners
of your passion and sprawl
in the light and shade of your valleys
reminding me clearly
distant sights
can easily become
explosions of a mood;

so let us ride along
through dewy midnights
dewy dawns
and tumble gently into
disemboweled noontides;

—you need not look just the way I want.

Somewhere

Somewhere a mother sobs
through bomb-shattered nights
hunger drains the blood of children.
Somewhere we eat the sputum of our pride
when we know nothing and we blunder.
Somewhere a woman sees her sick man
teeter on the edge of midnight
and turn his back to her and all forever.
Somewhere in the arena we lose our heads
amid the boos and jeers and whoops
along the sidelines.
Somewhere a mother awaits
her man, her son
in chains of an oppressor
or waits for those who never come
and still endures we know not how.
And yet amid the smoking debris
of a fear-driven world
while man juggles with megaton eggs,
somewhere a woman gives the world an artist:
a child who sings and dances,
dreams and weaves a poem round the universe
plunging down the womb
to fire a cell
sinking down a borehole
to probe the spring of life
from where the earth will rise
to meet the sky.
Somewhere in ancient China, it is told,
a man made a song
out of the wailing of a dove
a song that moved all animals
to rise and kill the serpent
who ate the bird's young ones.

To know our sorrow
is to know our joy—
Somewhere a mother will rejoice.

MBUYISENI OSWALD MTSHALI

Mbuyiseni Oswald Mtshali achieved critical acclaim for his best-selling book of poems *Sounds of a Cowhide Drum*, first published in South Africa and republished in England. He was born in 1940 in Vryheid, Natal, South Africa. Educated at Inkamana High School and, for two years, the University of South Africa, he finished college at the New School for Social Research in New York, majoring in English and education. He has worked at menial jobs, including messenger, laborer, copywriter, clerk, and driver, and as a journalist, writing for the *Rand Daily Mail* and the *Star*. He has published two books of poems, *Sounds of a Cowhide Drum* and *Fireflames*. He is Deputy Headmaster of Pace Commercial College in Soweto.

The Birth of Shaka

His baby cry
was of a cub
tearing the neck
of the lioness
because he was fatherless.

The gods
boiled his blood
in a clay pot of passion
to course in his veins.

His heart was shaped into an ox shield
to foil every foe.

Ancestors forged
his muscles into
thongs as tough
as wattle bark

and nerves
as sharp as
syringa thorns.

His eyes were lanterns
that shone from the dark valleys of Zululand
to see white swallows
coming across the sea.
His cry to two assassin brothers:
"Lo! you can kill me
but you'll never rule this land!"

Shaka was the famous and great nineteenth-century Zulu Emperor who resisted
white encroachment into his empire in South Africa.

Amagoduka at Glencoe Station

We traveled a long journey
through the wattle forests of Vryheid,
crossed the low-leveled Blood River,
whose water flowed languidly
as if dispirited by the
shattered glory of my ancestors.

We passed the coal fields of Dundee—
blackheads in the wrinkled face
of Northern Zululand—
until our train ultimately came
to a hissing stop at Glencoe.

Many people got off,
leaving the enraged train

to snort and charge at the night
on its way to Durban.

The time was 8:oo p.m.

I picked up my suitcase;
sagging under the weight of a heavy overcoat,
I shambled to the "Non-European Males" waiting room.

The room was crowded,
the air hung, a pall of choking odor,
rotten meat, tobacco and sour beer.

Windows were shut tight
against the sharp bite of winter.

Amagoduka sat on bare floor,
their faces sucking the warmth
of the coal fire crackling in the corner.

They chewed dried bread,
scooped corned beef with rusty knives,
and drank *mqomboti* from the plastic can
which they passed from mouth to mouth.

They spoke animatedly
and laughed in thunderous peals.

A girl peeped through the door;
they shuddered at the sudden cold blast,
jumped up to fondle and leer at her,
"*Hau! ngena Sisi!*"—"Oh! come in sister!"

She shied like a frightened filly
banged the door and bolted.
They broke into a tumultuous laughter.

One of them picked up a guitar,
plucked it with broken fingernails,
caressed its strings with a castor-oil bottle—

it sighed like a jilted girl.
"You play down! *Phansi!* Play D," he whispered.

Another joined in with a concertina;
its sound fluttered in flowery notes
like a butterfly picking pollen from flower to flower.

The two began to sing,
their voices crying for the mountains
and the hills of Msinga, stripped naked of
their green garment.

They crossed rivers and streams,
gouged dry by the sunrays,
where lowing cattle genuflected
for a blade of grass and a drop of water
on riverbeds littered with carcasses and bones.

They spoke of hollow-cheeked maidens
heaving drums of brackish water
from a faraway fountain.

They told of big-bellied babies
sucking festering fingers
instead of their mothers' shriveled breasts.

Two cockroaches
as big as my overcoat buttons
jived across the floor,
snatched meat and bread crumbs
and scurried back to their hideout.

The whole group joined in unison:
curious eyes peered through frosted windows,
"*Ekhaya bafowethu!*"—"Home brothers."

We come from across the Tugela River,
we are going to Egoli! Egoli! Egoli!
where they will turn us into moles
that eat the gold dust
and spit out blood.

We'll live in compounds
where young men are pampered
into partners for older men.

We'll visit shebeens
where a whore waits for a fee
to leave your balls burning
with syphilitic fire.

If the gods are with us—
Oh! beloved black gods of our forefathers,
What have we done to you,
Why have you forsaken us—
We'll return home
to find our wives nursing babies—
unknown to us
but only to their mothers and loafers.

Amagoduka is a Zulu term for mine laborers.
Mqomboti is a South African home brew. Egoli is the Zulu name for Johannesburg
(literally, "the city of gold").

The Raging Generation

Babies of yesterday,
children of today,
adults of tomorrow
ripening overnight like grapes in an untended vineyard—
I salute you with languorous words of pretense;
I drink the bitterness in the calabashes of your hearts.
The pouches of your cheeks are full of boiling tears,
there is broiling blood in the goatskin purses
in your unpummeled souls.

    Men children in the promised land of your forefathers,
    returning swallows who presage the coming
      of our summers,
    the bane of the receding winters of our oppression,
    unbroken steeds, whose hooves raised the dust
    of Soweto streets,
    where your maimed bodies were cut down by
      doom-primed fire shells
    from depraved barrels,
    little girls, budding flowers of our youth,
    your tight inviolate virginal veil torn asunder
    by the wanton penis of the monster.

Mothers and fathers of the days that lie ahead
like a carpet of choice velvet,
your eyes are the beams
that see the glorious future
that lies ahead
beyond the swirling streams of scarlet waves.

    I salute your fearlessness;
    I stand in awe of your bravery,
    and I bend my knee at the shrine of your steadfastness.

I hear your heart-touching songs at the memorial services
where you celebrate the passing of your comrades.

Amandla! Amandla! Amandla! Ngawethu!
Power! Power! Power! To the people!

Weep Not for a Warrior

A warrior drinks the goat's blood for bravery
as a willow in a swamp sucks water
to grow stalwart and stay ever green.

A warrior never perishes;
he is sustained by the glorious deeds of the departed;
he eats the raw meat of fearlessness
and awaits his canonization in the realm of heroes,
where all the freedom fighters dwell;
their numerous names are inscribed for posterity
in the massive girth of the baobab tree.

Fear has no roots
strong enough to pierce
the armored heart of a man in bondage,
whose unbridled anger tears the tiger from its lair,
grabs the lion by the tail,
spears the elephant on its trunk.

Tears were not made
to fall like rain on the grave of the warrior,

to drown the indomitable spirit,
and wash away his halo of martyrdom.

As the clouds of war gather,
and the southern sky frowns with rage,
and the mountains quiver like broth,
and the lightning swords the firmament,
and the clouds melt into cascades of water,
and the gushing torrents collect the corpses
and flush them like logs into a raging sea,
the death knell will echo to every corner.

The warrior will lie there, solemn
in his impregnable casket.
His proud widow and children will say,
   "Weep not for him,
   He was a brave warrior;
   Let him rest on the buffalo-hide bed,
   where his forefathers repose."

Nightfall in Soweto

Nightfall comes like
a dreaded disease
seeping through the pores
of a healthy body
and ravaging it beyond repair.

A murderer's hand,
lurking in the shadows,

clasping a dagger,
strikes down the helpless victim.

I am the victim.
I am slaughtered
every night in the streets.
I am cornered by the fear
gnawing at my timid heart;
in my helplessness I languish.

Man has ceased to be man,
Man has become beast,
Man has become prey.

I am the prey;
I am the quarry to be run down
by the marauding beast
let loose by cruel nightfall
from his cage of death.

Where is my refuge?
Where am I safe?
Not in my matchbox house
where I barricade myself against nightfall.

I tremble at his crunching footsteps,
I quake at his deafening knock at the door.
"Open up!" he barks like a rabid dog
thirsty for my blood.

ARTHUR NORTJE

Arthur Nortje was born in 1942 in Cape Province, South Africa. After graduating from Belleville "Colored" University College, he taught in Port Elizabeth. In 1965 he went to Jesus College, Oxford, from which he received a B.A. and a Ph.B. in English. He taught in Canada before returning to England, where he died suddenly in December 1970. According to Dennis Brutus, his eighth-grade teacher, Nortje was the most talented of the new generation of South African poets. He was a prizewinner in the Mbari Poetry Competition in 1962. Brutus has edited a posthumous volume of his poetry, *Dead Roots*.

Midnight

Tonight, precisely at that wall
my room's floor pauses in its walk,
throws up a gaze, observes the clock.
Bulb and brandy begin to talk.

Energy flows and sounds emerge,
but not from me—some alien source.
Beyond glass panels at my door
the darkness grins with utter force.

It creaked, the room's one empty chair:
devil or angel on my seat?
Outside my window, lamps bead blood
down on a tired waiting street.

The toilet gurgles by my ear,
sucks someone's paper down the drain.
Its chain keeps keeping vigilance
on odors of bowels, odors of pain.

Night after night I lie and wait
for sleep's return, but she, but she
is gripped in spastic fists of fear,
trembling at noises made by me.

South Africa, 1961

Soliloquy: South Africa

It seems me speaking all the lonely time,
whether of weather or death in winter,
or, as you expected and your eyes asked, love,
even to the gate where good-bye could flame it.
The last words that issue from the road
are next day regretted because meant so much.

All one attempts is talk in the absence
of others who spoke and vanished
without so much as an echo.
I have seen men with haunting voices
turned into ghosts by a piece of white paper,
as if their eloquence had been black magic.

Because I have wanted so much, your you,
I have waited hours and tomorrows, dogged
and sometimes doggish but you often listened.
Something speaks on when something listens:
in a room a fly can be conversation,
or a moth which challenges light but suffers.

Should you break my heart open, revive the muscle
for March grows on with mounting horror:

how to be safe is our main worry.
To keep you happy I shall speak more,
though only in whispers of freedom
now that desire has become subversive.

The gulls are screaming. I speak out to sea.
Waters, reared for attack, break forward:
without a word, this violence. From the cliffs
above the warm, shark-breeding sea that drowns
the oracle of the vibrant air I walk
and hear the ropes that thrash against the flagpoles.

The wind's voice moans among the willows.
Would you say that air can move so much?
It echoes so much of ourselves. In you
lies so much speech of mine buried
that for memory to be painless I must knife it.
It seems me speaking all the lonely time.

Cape Town, 1963

Brief Thunder at Sharpeville

Because one dead man does not make a summer
there are black hands in the sky that clamor,
faces that coolly stare from the concrete gloom.
Of my kind are many willing and able
to suffer the truncheon, to puzzle the jackboot.

Patrol this limbo day that swarms with people,
I being one of them. Meanwhile the sky,

grown grey with waiting, rumbles impatiently.
Clouds steel themselves for battle, which is common,
& clouds can never quarrel without weeping.

A squall of blobbing rain. Short argument,
stuttered out like gunfire;
So air is acrid with smoke & soil damp with blood.
Dead streets I notice, & not with terror:
I came out living. Of me there are many.

4/64

Letter from Pretoria Central Prison

The bell wakes me at 6 in the pale spring dawn
with the familiar rumble of the guts negotiating
murky corridors that smell of bodies. My eyes
find salutary the insurgent light of distances.
Water drops rain crystal cold; my wet
face in ascent from an iron basin
greets its rifled shadow in the doorway.

They walk us to the workshop. I am eminent,
the blacksmith of the block: these active hours
fly like sparks in the furnace; I hammer metals
with zest, letting the sweating muscles
forge a forgetfulness of worlds more magnetic.
The heart, being at rest, life peaceable,
your words filter softly through my fibers.

Taken care of, in no way am I unhappy,
being changed to neutral. You must decide
today, tomorrow, bear responsibility,
take gaps in pavement crowds, refine ideas.
Our food we get on time. Most evenings
I read books, Jane Austen
for elegance, agreeableness (*Persuasion*).

Trees are green beyond the wall, leaves through the mesh
are cool in sunshine
among the monastic white flowers of spring that float
prematurely across the exercise yard, a square
of the cleanest stone I have ever walked on.
Sentinels smoke in their boxes, the wisps
Curling lovely through the barbed wire.

Also music and cinema, yesterday double feature.
At 4:00 p.m. it's back to the cell; don't laugh
to hear how accustomed one becomes. You spoke
of hospital treatment—I see the smart nurses
bringing you grapefruit and tea—good
luck to the troublesome kidney.
Sorry there's no more space. But date your reply.

August 1966

All Hungers Pass Away

All hungers pass away,
we lose track of their dates:

desires arise like births,
reign for a time like potentates.

I lie and listen to the rain
hours before full dawn brings
forward a further day and winter sun
here in a land where rhythm fails.

Wanly I shake off sleep,
stare in the mirror with dream-puffed eyes:
I drag my shrunken corpulence
among tables of rich libraries.

Fat hardened in the mouth,
famous viands tasted like ash:
the mornings-after of a sweet escape
ended over bangers and mash.

I gave those pleasures up,
the sherry circuit, arms of a bland girl;
Drakensberg lies swathed in gloom,
starvation stalks the farms of the Transvaal.

What consolation comes
drops away in bitterness.
Blithe footfalls pass my door
as I recover from the wasted years.

The rain abates. Face-down
I lie, thin arms folded, half aware
of skin that tightens over the pelvis.
Pathetic, this, the dark posture.

Oxford, November 1970

SIPHO SEPAMLA

Sipho Sepamla is a poet, short-story writer, editor, and teacher who works as Personnel Officer for an East Rand company. He is Editor and Publisher of *Sketch*, a drama journal, was Publisher of the now-defunct *New Classic*, and is on the editorial board of the revived journal *The Classic*. He has published three books of poems: *Hurry Up to It!*, *The Blues Is You in Me*, and *The Soweto I Love*, poems based on the Soweto Riots of June 1976; and a novel, *A Ride on the Whirlwind*. He is an acknowledged master of satire and irony.

The Will

The house, by right,
you will have to vacate
surrender the permit
and keep your peace

The burglar-proofing and the gate
will go to my elder son
so will the bicycle
and a pair of bracelets

The kitchen-scheme and utensils
will go to my little girl
so will the bathtub
and the two brooms

The bedroom suite
will go to my younger son
who is married
so will the studio couch

The peach tree uproot
it might grow in the homelands
so might it be with your stem

The Bible
you will have to share
for you will always want its light

The cat spotted black and white
you will have to divide
for that you'll need God's guidance.

Soweto

I have watched you grow
like fermented dough
and now that you overflow the bowl
I'm witness to the panic you have wrought

you were born an afterthought
on the bypaths of highways
and have lived a foster child
whose wayward ways have broken hearts
the myths attending your name
have been spooks in the minds of many

your sons have been legendary
whose strength of character
has been a cause of pride

but you too have known shadows of men
who scurry and scuttle at every beck and call
in search of substantials

you have been a huge quiet cemetery
where many have been buried by day
resurrected by night
to make calls at night-vigils
of mothers you have made widows
who had to gird loins
to take on men's tasks

you have made of mourning
a way of life
the flowers that adorn your face
were born by mothers in grief

you have been a bad dream
which gnawed at the conscience of some
until averted eyes looked on
at the teeming of beings

there have been times
the incisions on your earlobes were misread
and those on your wrists abused
there have been times
the song from a thousand of your voices
was heard as a discord
and the dance of a million of your feet
was said to be off the beat

on your neck was placed a yoke of laws
which have tried to strangle your life
and once you strained muscles
to shake off the restraints
a great roar went up abroad

I love you, Soweto
I've done so long before
the summer swallow deserted you
I have bemoaned the smell of death
hanging on your other neck like an albatross
I have hated the stench of your blood
blood made to flow in every street

but I have taken courage
in the thought that
those who mother your back
will carry on with the job
of building anew
a body of being
from the ashes in the ground

Tell Me News

Tell me of a brother
who hanged himself in prison
with a blanket
was he punch-drunk

Tell me of a brother
who flung himself to death
from the ninth floor of a building
did his grip fumble with the loneliness up there

Tell me of a hooded man
who picked out others of his blood on parade
was his skin beginning
to turn with solitude

Oh, tell me of a sister
who returned home pregnant
from a prison cell
has she been charged under the Immorality Act

Tell me of a brother
who hanged himself in jail
with a piece of his torn pair of jeans
was he hiding a pair of scissors in the cell

Tell me, tell me, sir
has the gruesome sight
of a mangled corpse
not begun to sit on your conscience

The Work Song

In Commissioner Street
On the Main Reef Road
In Prince's Avenue
Down there where people are
I've heard the anguish of a chant
Heard rising into the air
Like orchestrated screams of a big band
The harmony of the laborer's voice
Singing:
 abelungu goddamn
 abelungu goddamn
 basibiza bojim
 basibiza bojim

I've seen an army of tattered arms
Swing sharply past the glint of the sun
The pickaxe leaping, lapping up the ground
Thudding into the stubborn earth
Echoes of hoarse, coarse, croaking pleas
Ringing:
>   *abelungu goddamn*
>   *abelungu goddamn*
>   *basibiza bojim*
>   *basibiza bojim*

I've listened to the whisper: *abelungu, abelungu*
Agony fading, cascading to a humming: *goddamn, goddamn*
Men have ambled
Bones creaking
Bodies reeking
To a mold of dug-out soil aching to sit
Seeking new horizons from the lips of a tin
Of a homemade brew:
>   wiping sweat goddamn
>   sniffling mucus goddamn
>   *abelungu goddamn*
>   *basibiza bojim*
>   *basibiza bojim*

I've watched on busy streets
Those hands wave at a girl strutting by
Tossing at her a chorus of shrill whistles
Voices bellowing a mighty laughter
Weaved a knot of love and lust
Fingers crossed:
>   *dudlu ngani goddamn*
>   *dudlu ngani goddamn*
>   *abelungu goddamn*
>   *abelungu goddamn*
>   *basibiza bojim*
>   *basibiza bojim*

Stirred into a consciousness
To celebrate the unsung man
I've walked away in disbelief
Admiring
Requiring
Enquiring
The balance of nature:
To crown the laborer with such moving harmony
Chanting:

> *abelungu goddamn*
> *abelungu goddamn*
> *basibiza bojim*
> *basibiza bojim*
> *abelungu goddamn!*

Abelungu goddamn / basibiza bojim ("The whites are damned / They call us Jim") is a work song well known throughout South Africa among mine workers and road gangs.

Pimville Station

On the one side
stood a ticket office
two poles overlooking it
one bringing light
the other a link with the world outside
both symbols of its higher status in the surroundings
Under the same roof
was a fish and chips shop
too busy frying to watch its smell
Behind it
was a sulky pair of toilets

The whole sight
was like a pregnant cockroach waiting expectantly

On the other side
languished
a ramshackle general dealer's
too old to care for its looks

The two sides were linked by a steel bridge
crouched over the single-track line
quizzically
like a hunchback resting elbows on a table

The platform looked like a street pavement
raised
waist-high
This was Pimville Station

As hundreds of passengers
jostled and scurried out of the fenced-in station yard
I came to understand the scene
on Noah's Ark
the day after the flood

The railway policeman on the beat
stood out in the crowd
like a lighthouse
He was always blowing hot and cold
to be at a pitch for arresting anyone

On and around the station
business was brisk:
peanut vendors
thugs frisking fellow-travelers
women roasting mealie cobs
and an herbalist brooding over a dry root

Each morning
before the eastern wink
could peek
into chinks of corrugated iron roofs
I would hear blinking in my sleep
a rumbling
as of agitated steel hoofs
the clank and clatter of rolling wheels
grousing about carriages
swaying under strain

Sometimes I heard
crammed passengers
chatter and grumble above others
bemoaning
increased house rents
early-morning house raids
and the sordid drunkenness of their neighbors

So many times have I thought
about the defiant stance
of a railway station in a Location
my very first experience of
what is permissively called:
separate and equal amenities!

Home

There's a time yes a time
I would have liked to say home
home even to rugged mountains
and trees huddled on hillsides
home to cupped lands but

how can I say this is home
when mother has to plug wounds dripping blood
with sweat-stained hands
when sister has to shield from bullets
breasts drooping squirting pain

how can I say home
where father sits with his head
dipped in despair
his vision blurred by indecision

how can I call this home
when others call it Doornkop Thornhill
Limehill or Vergenoeg

how come this home
has become a dungeon
rewombing its children without qualms

how can this be home
where graves grow fast
and the people's minds are stunted by intrigue

I seek a care-less home
home to my heart's content
home

JAKI SEROKE

Jaki Seroke is a young poet who worked as an editor for Ravan Press on Staffrider books and *Staffrider* magazine in which his poems have been published. He has also been editor of the *Classic*. He lives in Thembisa Township, Johannesburg.

Era

some were engirthed with a canopy
of remorse some among us cried
like crocodiles some listened to the hokum
of "instigators and tomato sauce" some
licked their fingers after a clutch

at the burnt bridge others immediately
dumped everything another slipped down
with the night other faces went
stony in twilight's eye yet
another preferred to *baas* this dragon's land

MONGANE WALLY SEROTE

Mongane Wally Serote was born in 1944 in Sophiatown,
Johannesburg, South Africa. He was educated in South Africa, in
Lesotho, at Columbia University in New York, from which he earned
an M.F.A. in creative writing. He has published four books of poetry:
Yakhal'inkomo, which was to establish him as the most intensely
lyrical of the new generation of South African poets, *Tsetlo, No Baby
Must Weep*, and *Behold Mama, Flowers*, and a novel, *To Every
Birth Its Blood*. His poems and short stories have appeared in *The
Classic*, in *Staffrider* in Johannesburg, and in journals in the United
States. He teaches at the University of Botswana, in Gaborone.

City Johannesburg

This way I salute you:
My hand pulses to my back trousers pocket
Or into my inner jacket pocket
For my pass, my life,
Jo'burg City.
My hand like a starved snake rears my pockets
For my thin, ever lean wallet,
While my stomach groans a friendly smile to hunger,
Jo'burg City.
My stomach also devours coppers and papers,
Don't you know?
Jo'burg City, I salute you;
When I run out, or roar in a bus to you,
I leave behind me, my love,
My comic houses and people, my dongas and my ever whirling
    dust,
My death,
That's as related to me as a wink to the eye.

Jo'burg City,
I travel on your black and white and roboted roads,
Through your thick iron breath, which you inhale,
At six in the morning and exhale from five noon.
Jo'burg City,
That is the time when I come to you,
When your neon flowers flaunt from your electrical wind,
That is the time when I leave you,
When your neon flowers flaunt their way through the falling
    darkness
On your cement trees.
And as I go back, to my love,
My dongas, my dust, my people, my death,
Where death lurks in the dark like a blade in the flesh,
I can feel your roots, anchoring your might, my feebleness
In my flesh, in my mind, in my blood,
And everything about you says it,
That, that is all you need of me.
Jo'burg City, Johannesburg,
Listen when I tell you,
There is no fun, nothing, in it,
When you leave the women and men with such frozen
    expressions,
Expressions that have tears like furrows of soil erosion,
Jo'burg City, you are dry like death,
Jo'burg City, Johannesburg, Jo'burg City.

Hell, Well, Heaven

I do not know where I have been,
But, Brother,
I know I'm coming.
I do not know where I have been,
But, Brother,
I know I heard the call.
Hell! where I was I cried silently
Yet I sat there until now.
I do not know where I have been,
But, Brother,
I know I'm coming:
I come like a tide of water now,
But oh! there's sand beneath me!
I do not know where I have been
To feel so weak, Heavens! so weary.
But, Brother,
Was that Mankunku's horn?
Hell! my soul aches like a body that has been beaten,
Yet I endured till now.
I do not know where I have been,
But, Brother,
I know I'm coming.
I do not know where I have been,
But, Brother
I come like a storm over the veld,
And oh! there are some stone walls before me!
I do not know where I have been
To have fear so strong like the whirlwind (will it be that brief?)
But, Brother,
I know I'm coming.
I do not know where I have been,
But, Brother,
Was that Dumile's figure?
Hell, my mind throbs like a heartbeat; there's no peace;

And my body of wounds—when will they be scars?—
Yet I can still walk and work and still smile.
I do not know where I have been
But, Brother,
I know I'm coming.
I do not know where I have been,
But, Brother,
I have a voice like the lightning—thunder over the mountains.
But oh! there are copper lightning conductors for me!
I do not know where I have been
To have despair so deep and deep and deep
But, Brother,
I know I'm coming.
I do not know where I have been
But, Brother,
Was that Thoko's voice?
Hell, well, Heavens!

Ofay-Watcher Looks Back

I want to look at what happened.
That done,
As silent as the roots of plants pierce the soil,
I look at what happened.
Whether above the houses there is always either smoke or dust,
As there are always flies above a dead dog.
I want to look at what happened.
That done,
As silent as plants show color: green,
I look at what happened

When houses make me ask: do people live there?
As there is something wrong when I ask: is that man alive?
I want to look at what happened.
That done,
As silent as the life of a plant that makes you see it,
I look at what happened
When knives creep in and out of people
As day and night into time.
I want to look at what happened.
That done,
As silent as plants bloom and the eye tells you: something has
    happened.
I look at what happened
When jails are becoming necessary homes for people,
Like death comes out of disease.

I want to look at what happened.

During Thoughts After Ofay-Watching

We are caught up in a turning tide,
The river flows, the river ebbs,
The bubbles form and burst
And foam oozes out of our scalps,
The turn is long, turn is wide,
Hands and minds retract, craving to touch,
There at the wide and long turning,
If the water is not red and salty,
The odor is there and our minds see crimson
In that long and wide turn

Of the river that flows and ebbs, dries to dust at times;
We are caught up in a turning tide,
Slow; taking its pace, slow;
Throbbing like the pulse of one dying,
The turning tide, we are caught up there
Where the waves break before they ripen,
Many will break there,
Many will not become waves, they will peep and perish,
There at the turning tide,
The many waves gasping, the bubbles bursting rapidly,
Like closing eyes,
One day we'll wake up,
And on the rocky cheeks of the bank there'll be huge droplets
    flowing
And the reeds of the river will be dry like skeleton bones;
And the river shall be heard,
Flowing, flowing on, and on.
The route will be long and straight,
The bubbles will burst, like eyes looking back,
But the river shall flow like the song of birds.

A Poem in Black and White

if i pour petrol on a white child's face
and give flames the taste of his flesh
it won't be a new thing
i wonder how i will feel when his eyes pop
and when my nostrils sip the smell of his flesh
and his scream touches my heart
i wonder if i will be able to sleep;

i understand alas i do understand
the rage of a white man pouring petrol on a black child's face
setting it alight and shooting him in a pretoria street,
pretoria has never been my home
i have crawled its streets with pain
i have ripped my scrotal sack at every door i intended entering in
that city
and jo'burg city has never seen me, has never heard me
the pain of my heart has been the issue of my heart
sung by me
freezing in the air
but who has not been witness to my smile?
yet, alexandra's night shadow is soaked and drips with my tears.

Heat and Sweat

For sisters and brothers who may be weary

so you keep looking back
if you did not listen when the past was breathing
the present erases your name
child don't let laughter from insane strangers snatch our faces
the present is surprised at our songs
it is shocked that we still walk the streets the way we do
lost as we are
torn and bewildered by the sounds of our names
it is surprised that though the sight of our eyes staggers
and though the gait of our shadows seems to limp
we still put brick on brick and tell our children stories
so you keep looking back

even when the darkness is so thick it could touch your eyeballs
even when the darkness is such a huge space
ready with an insatiable thirst, swallowing, and even ready still
   to swallow
the last red drop that trickles still from your little heart,
don't you hear the songs
they can live in the present if we let them
these songs have a prowess of our mother's back
and the eloquence of our grandmother's foresight
about the time that never was
and the earth whose rhythm is an intoxicated dizziness
child
feel the wall while you walk and hold, hold
glue your eye into the distance and keep walking
move, child, move
if we don't get there
nobody must . . .

New York 1975

JAMES TWALA

James Twala, who lives in the Meadowlands section of Soweto, has had his poetry published in *Staffrider* magazine.

Biltong

The lean strips hang like
Dead faceless serpents on the slack washing line,
Waving like pliable branches.
The sun parches the biltong
With the patience of a housewife
And the wings of large flies
Sing continuously around the dangling strips
That are streaked with dark fat.

At dusk,
A large-mouthed woman emerges
From the house and stomps to the washing line,
Snaps at the jerking biltong
As if it were bait,
And plucks the biltong like dry
Washing from the washing line.

Inside the house
Four mounds of steaming porridge are ready,
And four lean-bodied children
Are squatting like sleepy frogs
With their eyes fixed on the biltong.

They gnaw on the biltong
With twisted faces,
Grip and tear the biltong

With their half-rotten teeth.
What is not ground well
Will be brought up
Deep in the night,
To be chewed a second time
Like cows in their kraal.

ZAMBIA

I don't see you these days
Let it be a better place where you are
A drunkard's loneliness awaits you here
Don't come—if they are improving you
                    —Richard A. Chima

Z AMBIAN WRITERS, like their eastern neighbors, are trying to confront and come to terms with a post-colonial situation and the realities of independence. Unlike Malawians, these poets operate within a very democratic system, which tolerates divergent opinions and constructive criticism of the social, economic, and political problems of their nation. Provided their writing does not advocate disunity, they are free to tackle any of the major problems—alcoholism, prostitution, inequalities between the haves and have-nots, corrupt and hypocritical leaders—but these themes find little treatment in serious poetry, which does not yet exist in any significant quantity.

However, some sensitive poets, including Richard Augustine Chima and Patu Simoko, once actively worked to prick the conscience of the nation. Chima, who defines poetry as the art of living and dying before a mirror, perceives his role as that of offering direction and consciousness-raising. In his handling of the themes of urban reality, the squalor and suffering of the working-class people who inhabit the ever-mushrooming slums and squatter compounds on the peripheries of the industrial centers, he parallels the performance of some of the best Angolan, Mozambican, and South African poets. More than anyone else in the volume, he completely identifies with the wretched of the earth; he assumes the persona and voice of a drunkard, a perfect mask for concealing his personality and exercising his freedom.

He intends, by writing verse, to drag society to the mirror in order to cleanse it of its falsehood. His metaphorical mirror figuratively describes the stylistic transparency and simplicity of his poetry, in which his readers are drawn to confront their own defaced faces. He employs sardonic humor, irony, and direct statement in a patently conversational style, delivering frontal attacks in a clear simple diction.

Chima is a poet with a good ear, capturing the racy and vibrant speech of the workers in the slum shebeens and city streets. His persona is a braggart with clear vision, whose voice is deceptively rough, but behind it is heard the voice of an ethical and morally astute individual, a sane and articulate seer. He is the shrewd, experienced fallen angel who knows all the corruption, hypocrisy, and scandal "up there," which he chronicles as he recounts his stories to fellow drunkards in the smoky, noisy, crowded shebeens at the "bottom," or to cellmates, the failures and the disillusioned victims of the rat race. He is an intensely lonely figure, aware of the acute blindness around him, and he speaks in urgent, imperative tones to try to stop destructive social trends.

Patu Simoko, who generally takes a panoramic view of the African continent, is stylistically less subtle than Chima. Thematically, his poems manifest the same concerns that preoccupy his colleague, as well as poets of Malawi and Zimbabwe, namely, the betrayal of promises, the corruption and the hypocrisy of the status quo and of top party leaders, who have transferred the revolution from the battlefield into the cities' bedrooms and hotel rooms and who enjoy comforts at the expense of the laboring masses they claim to represent. His favorite stylistic device is a combination of rhetorical questions and direct, accusatory statements that, through listing and cataloguing, work up to a cumulative climax. His voice is always raised, loud but without a tinge of real anger, as he chides the "beautifools" who pay lip service to black pride and African culture but are actually neck-deep in Western culture. In some cases, his voice is even celebratory, but his diction is simple, straightforward, and accessible, like that of most of the poetry in this collection.

In spite of the immense freedom that Zambians enjoy, their poetry is experiencing a stunted growth, and the few poets who have published volumes of their poetry have, curiously, fallen silent after their initial projects. Of these, Lyson Tembo's *Poems* (1972), Richard Chima's *The Loneliness of a Drunkard* (1973), and Patu Simoko's *Africa Is Made of Clay* (1975), all published in Lusaka, are perhaps the most significant.

Some thematic affinity with Malawian poetry exists only in the sense that, like Malawians, Zambian poets are dealing largely with post-colonial experience. In their moral stance and attitude toward suffering and the hardships that working people face in the slums, however, their poetry shares some of the attributes of the entire region's poetry. But because of the tolerance, as well as the freedom of expression, they enjoy, they are not compelled to express their protest in condemnatory tones.

RICHARD AUGUSTINE CHIMA

Richard Augustine Chima was born on August 10, 1945, in Zambia. He was educated at Evelyn Hone College of Applied Arts and Commerce, in Lusaka, and at the South West London College, in England, where he earned the Higher Diploma of Chartered Secretaries. He has held responsible positions in Television Zambia and has served as Company Secretary for the Industrial Development Corporation (Indeco) and the Kariba North Bank Hydro-Electric Power Project and as Deputy General Manager of the Kapiri Glass Factory in Kabwe, Zambia. He is Chief Projects Officer for the Commonwealth Fund for Technical Co-operation in London. He was a pioneer Zambian poet. His volume of verse, *The Loneliness of a Drunkard*, was first published in 1973 and was issued in a revised edition in 1978.

Chronique Scandaleuse

I am the leaf that fell—from the top
You see, up there, is everything—because
   they are few.
The principle is: the bottom is always crowded
   except in queues,
The ceilings are make-believe to any of the
   lower crowds.

Now if you don't meet me with my toolbox
   at the midnight hour
Then I will have taken up residence at the
   central prison.
I always see a taxpayer who is heavily projecting
   benefits.
He flew an entire ship to the moon—to find
   nothing.

I am working on the back door of this bank.
The door is stubborn.
As said, no courage so bold as that forced by
   utter desperation.
All progress started with crime.
"The greatest risk of all
   is the acquisition of capital,"
A cellmate said one day.
   Today society approved his hanging.

When you die
No heaven issues refunds of life
Only complete blackouts!

1968

In This Shanty Shebeen Without You

I don't see you these days
Let it be a better place where you are
A drunkard's loneliness awaits you here
Don't come—if they are improving you

I am measuring this deteriorating scene
It is funny we die slowly here
This bar is sure empty without you
All those singsongs together
The enchanting spirit—they left with you

They clean mirrors—most clean
The service is still staggering
We all smoke—our faces squeezed cloudy
No one knows you left—are you improved?

I slept on my stool the entire weekend last
I passed out, they had to wipe my face with ice
It was unnecessary aid—they knew it
They wanted to celebrate my coming around
Illusions are more comfortable than reality
(They are nice ones here too)

You want to be cared for
And to be played with
Seduce me—to this adventure
But he who drinks has the only power

Talking about stopping is habit-forming
I drink, I want even drugs legalized too
They send policemen here not doctors
Now you are with them—tell them what we
    want!
Our roof is a sky full of stars.
Seize opportunity
Stay as sweet as you are
Don't let this separate us
In this bar I remain
Without you but a little

They will only increase but not satisfy—
Your human escalating expectations
(At aerodynamic speeds)
Don't come—if they are improving you
I will meet you in my constantly postponed
    future

I am a busy man since you left
In this great panoramic parade of life
I took a trip round your image late last session
I collided with myself
Because I used up all the circle
Come and see how you have overvacuumed
The real environment available
But honestly
Don't come
If they have improved you.

1969

Why?

I see a world torn apart
By an attitude which is old
As it has been through all eternity.
Your kind is your enemy.

The store is stockpiled with wars
Requisitions are made against it.
The store's clerks, as it is,
Wonder why, are highest paid.

Give me a balance sheet of the entire world
Your profit account underlined.
I want poor souls too
To see the modern Roman Will
They mistakenly cry for.

Workers and peasants
Stop displaying your ribs;
Eat cakes.

1968

PATU SIMOKO

Patu Simoko was born in 1951 in a village in Petauke District, eastern Zambia. He attended Chassa Secondary School, St. Paul's Secondary School, in Kabwe, and Evelyn Hone College of Applied Arts and Commerce, in Lusaka, from which he obtained a diploma in journalism in 1971. He has worked as news reporter for the *Times of Zambia, Zambia Daily Mail,* the *East African Standard* and the *Daily Nation* in Nairobi, and the *Daily News* and *Sunday News* in Dar es Salaam. Between 1977 and 1979 he studied political science and public administration by correspondence course. He covered the Angolan civil war in 1976. A former Journalism Lecturer at Evelyn Hone, he also worked as Communications Officer for the Housing Project Unit of the World Bank in Lusaka before assuming his present position as Political Correspondent for the *Times of Zambia*. He has published a volume of poetry, *Africa Is Made of Clay*, and two other books.

Africa Is Made of Clay

africa is made of clay
she breaks, balanced on heads too proud.
i've heard the voices of the marchers
shouting "black is beautiful,"
they put wigs where should have stayed pots
full of black milk and honey;
they shouted "black 'n' proud"
and their voices were made of lipstick.
they marched:

africa's nice, we're right, this being night
africa's nice, we're right, this being night.

but, brother, take away your africa.
africa is mud thatched with grass,
she catches fire and burns to ash.
she cries for pride more bitter than songs
of the proud black and the beautifools.
africa is clay,
she breaks in the violence of the storm;
africa is the storm breaking her own pots.
africa is made of clay.

© 1977 Patu Simoko. Reprinted from *Africa Is Made of Clay*.

Did We Laugh or Did We Cry?

mother, did we laugh or did we cry?
ah, there are silent whispers of a people embattled;
voices crashed into blood with the taste of freedom
our hearts shouted No to colony seekers
our arms threw independence stones
we fought
we won.
did we cry
over memories of lost blood?
did we laugh
promising ourselves better tomorrows?
we still remember the smiles of victory
sweetening the agonies of yesterday
whereafter the sons of our huts
stood unrepentant on platforms
where they built for us schools in their minds
hospitals on their tongues
and tarred roads on their feet.

today we sit here mother to son
under fallen rostrums and crushed dreams
calling the names of the same old witch doctors
walking the paths of the forests
and growing too old for late schools.

nothing has changed!

Corruption

africa.
how many faces did i see in the mirror of your dawn?
how many voices hung true on your mouth?
few leaders slept out last night and
deprived the beneficiaries of your freedom.
the freeman has returned repeating songs of the battlefield
where ago he fought the sun and made rain;
then you bathed in freedom, giving him excess glory.
but africa's patriots plotted again last night,
for you lie in the sleep of one milked and barren,
covered in fallen leaves
under a tree with neither shadow nor soul.
the freeman, embittered, has returned to the battlefield
to fill rivers of sodom and gomorrah.
was it europe who clung to your breasts
and broke your thighs from the erection?
was it one of your front men
who drank more than a soldier's drink?

silent continent,
your eyes are turned
your tongue is forked
your lips are bent
and my spear is bent on more struggle!

ZIMBABWE

My limbs will never be shackled.
The cock has crowed: the day has come!
Awake, my son! Arise and walk!
　　　　　—Mudereri Kadhani

"IN OUR LAND / Bullets are beginning to flower," wrote Jorge Rebelo, the Mozambican poet, and there is no more appropriate metaphor to concretize the cultural renaissance in independent Zimbabwe, a process stimulated by the protracted armed struggle. The relaxation of the stringent censorship regulations and the restoration of basic human rights to the black majority have resulted in a cultural flowering in music, dance, art, and literature. The country's black poets, no longer obscure and isolated, can now freely publish works they composed during the colonial period, some of which are included in this collection. In these poems there are striking resemblances to other protest poems from the subcontinent, despite the fact that they were written in a closed society.

Thematically, black Zimbabwean poetry bears great similarities to the anticolonial poetry of Angola and Mozambique. Thematic parallels with black South African poetry reflect common experiences under a system modeled on the apartheid plan. Like their counterparts to the south, black Zimbabwean poets protest against the exploitation of African laborers by white masters ("The Factory Hands"), political detention ("In the Zoo," "If I Leave Here Alive"), police brutality and excesses ("Raid on the Market"), circumscription ("The Curfew Breakers"), the victimization, humiliation, and general oppression of the silent majority ("I Love"), and, like their Namibian colleagues, they contrast the comfort and luxury the white people enjoy with the squalor and misery into which their African neighbors are shunted ("Circular Roads"). Other poems deal with the theme of the armed struggle itself, celebrating, as in "Rekayi Tangwena," some heroic figures who defied and resisted eviction from their ancestral homelands.

However, unlike their Angolan and Mozambican colleagues under similar conditions, some black Zimbabwean poets show a rare sensitivity to the complex and confused situation in their country during the days of the "internal" settlement. This is revealed in poems such as "Important Matters," "Revolution," and "The Redeemer," which treat the theme of false leadership also encountered in Malawian and Zambian poetry.

Stylistically, although there is no absolute uniformity, the poems are unadorned, their diction is simple and straightforward, and the language is generally accessible, pared down, and dwelling on immediate details, which crystallize into vivid images. The stark imagery of Polycarp Chimedza's "Raid on the Market" recalls the visual-aural imagery in Dennis Brutus's "The Sounds Begin Again," as well as that in many poems by South African poets Mbuyiseni Oswald Mtshali, Mongane Wally Serote, and Sipho Sepamla. Many of the poets tend to use short sentences, in well-controlled and balanced forms. For the most part, the terse direct statement is preferred to the elaborate one, and sometimes the poets fuse formal with colloquial language and weave ritual chants, proverbs, and elements of folk tales into the fabric of their poems, a common stylistic practice in Malawian poetry. Symbols drawn from the Zimbabwean landscape, especially rocks, mountains, and ruins, are also prevalent in these poems. Irony and wit are favored by many of the poets, who use them with disarming effect.

The tone of much of this poetry, unlike that of neighboring Mozambique, Angola, and even South Africa, is amazingly somber, the anger tempered by sardonic humor. This poetry has more tonal affinities with Malawian poetry than with the rest of the poetry in this collection. Usually there is no shouting here; the anger is quiet, carefully controlled, but nevertheless unrelenting. In some poems, for instance "Rekayi Tangwena," there is a greater modulation of tone, from the reverent and supplicatory, since the speaker addresses the hero, to the challenging and threatening, when the hero addresses shadowy enemies, to affectionate, as he responds to the poem's speaker. Since the poems' audiences are usually fellow Zimbabweans, the poets' adoption of such somber tones is understandable.

There is currently a literary deluge in Zimbabwe, with Harare and Gweru fast becoming the centers of publishing in independent Central Africa. Two anthologies of poetry have so far been published in Zimbabwe, one edited by Kizito Muchemwa, *Zimbabwean Poetry in English* (1978), and the other edited by Mudereri Kadhani and Musaemura Zimunya, *And Now the Poets Speak: Poems Inspired by the Struggle for Zimbabwe* (1981). The poets themselves have been active in bringing out individual volumes, the most noteworthy being Samuel Chimsoro's *Smoke and Flames*, Mudereri Kadhani's *Quarantine Rhythms*, and *The Milkman Doesn't Only Deliver Milk*, by Charles Mungoshi, one of the leading novelists and short-story writers using both Shona and English. Musaemura Zimunya, perhaps the leading poet of the country, published two volumes of his poetry in 1982, *Thought-Tracks* and *Kingfisher, Jikinya and Other Poems*. In addition to the books, they continue to publish individual poems in such local journals as *Two Tone* and *Chirimo* as well as abroad.

It is to be hoped that with independence these poets will continue to be the conscience of their new nation and with their self-critical attitude provide insights into the problems of their country and region.

POLYCARP CHIMEDZA

Polycarp Chimedza is a young Zimbabwean poet who fled his country in 1977 and traveled to the United States via Botswana for further studies. He lived in Maryland. Mbulelo Mzamane, a South African writer, who met him in Gaberone in 1977, supplied these poems. Mzamane says he appeared to be about eighteen years old.

The Factory Hands

Hopes are pedaled along the rioting tarmac
Sustaining sparks of a horizontal existence;
The factory hands grapple with the wild throbbing pistons
For a few hard-sweated coins, while
The bespectacled specter sits in air-conditioned languor
And proclaims, "Production must be increased."
The grief-wrung minds are shuttled
Between the agony of the factory
And the misery at home.

August 1975

Raid on the Market

The sirens slice the afternoon air,
And jackboots strike the dull tarmac;
Conversations are stilled in birth;
Transactions cease and laughter stalls,
Screams choke behind gaping mouths,
And hearts wring with sudden adrenaline.

Naked feet drum in desperate flight,
Wailing babies rock in humid jerks,
And fear is mouthed in multiple bursts.
Citrons football, football along the ocher dust,
Yellow fingers strike the air and splatter,
Tomatoes gape—surprised by the sudden fall,
As silver bracelets are liberally handed out.

August 1975

SAMUEL CHIMSORO

Samuel Chimsoro was born on February 13, 1949, at Murewa, Zimbabwe. He was educated at Chitate Magaya School, Mutasa Government School, Nyatsime College (secondary education), and Fletcher High School in Gweru. He was trained as a laboratory technician at the Salisbury Polytechnic in Harare from 1971 to 1976. He works as a Civil Engineering Technician in a government radiation detection laboratory. His poems have been published in local Zimbabwean journals and the anthology *And Now the Poets Speak*. He has published a volume of poetry, *Smoke and Flames*, and a novel, *Nothing Is Impossible*, is forthcoming.

The Curfew Breakers

to walk in the sun
hoe in hand,
to dig drains
and engrave sorrow
on anthills
is for the love of life.

to sweep the streets
and fence the gates,
to keep next of kin informed that
the right of admission
into the sun
is reserved
is for the love of life.

to turn to moonlight
for reflections of warmth,
to dance to drums
barefooted

and sanctify the earth
as the dust of ancestors
is freed from the earth
is for the love of life.

to sleep
on the skeletons
of fallen stars
and dream that
the right of admission
into the darkness
is reserved
is for the love of life.

to wake up in the morning
as an object of dispute
and die in the evening
as a curfew breaker
is also for the love of life.

I Love

I love the silent majority
That rise earlier than the sun
To a breakfast of expectations.

I love the silent majority
Whose bread eaters raise their eyes
To sensitize the breadwinners' backs
To their nudging anxieties.

I love the silent majority
For whom givers maximize
Fringe benefits with a whip
To sensitize the receivers' backs
To the costs of classes and races.

I love the silent majority
That for a week, a month, a century
Welcomes the empty-handed householder
Who nurtures them on hope
For their strength to sleep.

I love the curfew breakers
Who offer morsels of prayers,
Whispering loving complaints
For which they rest in peace
Beneath the feet of a sick society
That turns to snores
The snorts of nestlings
Mourning their deported householders.

I love the silent majority
That will rise earlier than the sun.

The Change

What used to be
A missionary's poker
Is now a scepter
Leaning against a sooted chimney.
The soft white wood
Has all burnt.
Its reluctant warmth is refuse
Diffused into the earth;
The grey covering ashy trash
Wanting to be blown.
What used to be
A gregarious row of chairs,
Docks and electric seats
Is now a row of stone
Round an outdoor fireplace
Loaded with mutsatsati logs.
The heat of riots is gone.
The heart of sermons is gone.
Speeches were concluded
Now speakers are redundant.
What used to be
So white is now all
In the museum of memory
While black hands dip
Lumps of their constitution
In the same soup bowl.

To Come Back Home

To come back home
    And find your pillow
        An anthill of ants
            That gnawed your
                father
                mother
                brother
                sister
Exhumes the agony
That sent you away
With a knotted promise
To come back home.

The Laborer

I

Nothing grows on the laborer's skin
But beads of volatile diamonds
While the whip on his back
Like the knife that cuts the crystals
Lends strength to necklaces
That hold their hypnotic glitter
By the landlady's breast

II

The laborer during his hot day
Wipes his crisps and jingles away

Like a mother wiping her appetite,
Like an anthill letting its food fly.

Yet sweating in the chili fields
Brings breaths of sugary dreams
That draw the laborer's tongue
To lick his dry and cracked lips
While the landlady sips her wine.

III

The laborer's dreams will not tell
The sour taste of grapes he sees
But the sweet taste of wine
Aging in the landlady's glass.

MUDERERI KADHANI

Mudereri Kadhani is a Zimbabwean poet who lived and studied in England until independence, when he returned to his native land. While in England he published a volume of poems, *Quarantine Rhythms*, and upon his return to Zimbabwe, he co-edited, with Musaemura Zimunya, an anthology of Zimbabwean poetry, *And Now the Poets Speak*.

Rekayi Tangwena

I

Blow one bred blow two, my friends
The third soon tumbled after that.
Blow three spawned the fourth, not so?
And that one hatched strike five, Great Beast.
As six runs often after five

So seven sired the eighth, watch out!
From eight to nine, where will it lead?
At ten it's ended; the game is up!

Tit for tat, a scratch proved a searing clout.
In which god's name does insolent orphan turn tyrant,
Does guest snatch to gobble the host's last morsel?

But come, old Father, peace we pray;
Stay your arm, Great Chief, and let it pass.
Have we not cheered till the sweat burst from our brows?
We heard and heeded, Father, your free words;
Rest now, rest now, rest, your sons have understood.

We cup our palms in tribute, Lord of the land,
Born when great Zambezi stirred, simmered, then boiled,
Hurling its rage over the riverbanks.

To this day your forehead gleams bright:
Was it not smeared with wax of the black wasp?
Our praise and thanks: a perfect emblem of courage
Cicatrized with the keenest gardenia thorn.
What fear then can there be of faltering?
So let this day release Zambezi's fury,
Let it burst banks, flood land, clear stumps.

Give me air! your hands smother my mouth.
Whose the crime if not the finger that poked the nest of the wasp?
If now you're stung and hurt, fool, don't whine you're wronged!
Clear the path! Let go my limbs!
Arrogant cheetah, when our roles are exchanged can you expect
That the vain spots on your coat will stay unstained?
Can the silence of the muzzled mouth not be heard?
So muzzled, how could I even breathe?
I choke! Let me draw breath!
Though you strive to thwart, I shall speak out!
Don't wink at me: we are not cousins.
Just let me be, let me walk on!

A wayfarer I shall rove through the land
With no rest till the family you scattered abroad
Is penned back in my fold.
I shall not be pinioned, elbow to knee.
I shall scour the land to provide for my sons;
Night and day I shall comb the forests.
In a deep refuge of rock I shall stow them away.
But when they emerge, beware their arrows!
Look out, wild predator who stirred the nest of the deadly wasp!

May my grin deceive you, child of snake,
For I shall haunt you, child of snake, night and day I shall hound
    you!
It is no idle threat: you remain my quarry to the end.
When tomorrow dawns all will be lost.

Up and away, my blood, my heirs,
Claim your birthright,
Rise up and follow!
Yes, Illustrious, your people acclaim you!
Can any stranger wear your name?

The call! the call! can you not hear the call
Of the forest, my lost ones?
Do not stifle what must be heard!
My limbs will never be shackled.
The cock has crowed: the day has come!
Awake, my son! Arise and walk!

III

Rekayi, Rekayi, to what are we called?
Rekayi, Rekayi, we entreat you for words!
Look how they have shattered your clan!
Can lightning strike on a cloudless day?
Speak, Rekayi, is it for us to look on helpless?
No, no, my sons, no!
The mountain is steep: we hazard our lives.
Once we were champions, well born and proud.
On now, my people! Can death be worse?

IV

Is it come to this, *Chirombowe*, living in caves,
Wild plums sustaining the son of a chief?
Is it come to this, Royal Blood, provoked like the wasp in her nest?
Tears rain down in a ceaseless drizzle;

Our children weep for the breast snatched from their lips;
Our chests are overburdened
With the fury of a beehive approached in daylight.
When, O when will you spell out our crime?
Our bowels are shriveled dust-dry
As crumbling maize cobs frizzled to cinders.
Famine plagues us like the ache of a diseased tooth,
Throttled we die like rats.
Like ripe potatoes hatching through ridges
Hunger leers from our lips chapped ashen-white.
Our cheeks cave in as seedlings wither through thirst.
Father, our throats are parched: Give us water!

V

No more, *Tavashasha*, enough now,
Tavashasha; your words are deeply implanted, Tavashasha!
Your sons come now to offer thanks.
We cry out, good father, our applause.
Over our hearts we have branded your name blood-red
Forever with the smoldering auger of our pride.

This soil: how it trembles to the firm tread of your steps.
This soil: familiar reed mat comforting sleep.
This soil: headrest of dreams, buttress of yearning.
This soil: the fruit of her breast is denied to none;
        the hungry she feeds with roots and wild
        plums;
        the thirsty drink at her springs.
This soil: asylum of a people,
        hearth where all grief is unloaded.

VI

No more, enough now, Great Champion,
Who in single combat won the war.

Your children cheer and clap their hands in thanks,
    Lord of the Wild.
But now do not stumble, we pray, Man of the Mountains.
Hammer of the snakes, give us arrows, give us eyes,
For today at least today we shall conquer.
We declare our strength and affirm our might!

Translated by George Faber. © 1978 Mudereri Kadhani. Reprinted from *Quarantine Rhythms*. By permission of Palladio Press.
Rekayi Tangwena, a heroic chief of the Ngwena people, challenged an eviction order for their removal from their ancestral homeland in northeastern Zimbabwe in the late 1960s in a protracted court case, which they eventually lost.
Chirombowe is a Shona term of respect for elders.
Tavashasha is another Shona term of respect for elders.

CHARLES MUNGOSHI

Charles Mungoshi was born on December 2, 1947, in Manyene Communal Area, Chivhu, Zimbabwe. He has published seven books in Shona and English. His first novel, *Makun'unu* (Heartbreak), won first prize in the 1968 Literature Bureau competition. *Coming of the Dry Season* was his first collection of short stories in English. In 1975 he won the Book Center (P.E.N.) Award for both Shona and English with two novels, *Ndiko Kupindana Kwamazuva* (How Time Passes) and *Waiting for the Rain*. The latter has been translated into Hungarian. A number of his poems have appeared in *Two Tone, Rhodesian Poetry in English 1977/78*, and *Zimbabwean Poetry in English*. His only book of poems, *The Milkman Doesn't Only Deliver Milk*, received the Longman-P.E.N. Award for the best English book of the year. He is Editor for Zimbabwe Publishing House, in Harare.

Important Matters

There are important matters on the agenda—
matters of life and death.
The gravity and importance of these matters
showed in our deeply furrowed faces
as we sat watching the empty throne
waiting for the chairman who was already hours late
to come and open the meeting
although each of us secretly felt and wished
he would come in and just say:
Call it a day, boys!

Hours later a messenger came in to say
the chairman had taken his girl
for a boat ride on Lake McIlwaine.

We sat hunched round the empty chair—
the day suddenly pulled from right under us.
There and then we began to plan an airtight plot
that would without fail bring about the downfall
of the chairman.
We looked at the plan from all angles
under all kinds of light
and when we were satisfied with it
we stepped out into the evening world
clutching our bags with faces that said:
It's been a trying day.

1975

If You Don't Stay Bitter for Too Long

If you don't stay bitter
and angry for too long
you might finally salvage
something useful
from the old country

a lazy half-sleep summer afternoon
for instance, with the whoof-whoof
of grazing cattle in your ears
tails swishing, flicking flies away
or the smell of newly turned soil
with birds hopping about
in the wake of the plough
in search of worms

or the pained look of your father
a look that took you all these years
and lots of places to understand

the bantering tone you used with your
grandmother and their old laugh
that said nothing matters but death

If you don't stay bitter
and angry for too long
and have the courage to go back
you will discover that the autumn smoke
writes different, more helpful messages
in the high skies of the old country.

1975

KIZITO Z. MUCHEMWA

Kizito Z. Muchemwa was born in 1950 at Mbedzi, Zimbabwe. He has an M.A. in English from the University of Zimbabwe and teaches at a secondary school in the Fort Victoria area. His poems have been published in *Rhodesian Poetry*, and he has compiled an anthology, *Zimbabwean Poetry in English*.

Tourists

They came into the wilderness, clichés in suitcases,
Talismans they cherished as shields against this poisonous madness
Lurking in the dark aggressive landscape of alienness.
Looking for recognition of this my dear land
They saw no familiar hills and heard no familiar songs.
Holding onto their fetishes they defy time and distance,
Send lines across oceans to tap the energies.
A faceless past economically nourishes wilting roots
Dying on the rocky exposures of understanding through fear.

They surround themselves with jacarandas and pines,
Build concrete walls around their homes.
I hope next time they will import snow, change
The reasons to humor their eccentric whims.

Already other trinkets hoot their mockery of our lives,
Proclaiming the raucous assertiveness of their makers.
But this land, this, the spirits dwelling in it,
Will not yield to such casual intimidation
Neither will it give out its rich sad secrets
To halfhearted tokens of transparent love.

1975

Circular Roads

Circular roads
eroded hillsides
going nowhere . . .

Colonial bungalows, wire-gauze windows
tropical verandas, Venetian blinds pathetically pretty
perched on wounded hillsides—facing nowhere . . .

Confusion of sinuous streams
hiding dirt in densely greened valleys
in kind seasons—sad beauty lies

broken in long forgotten railway lines,
puffing asthmatic minarets—mushrooms
sown by a drunken sower—

Tarred funereal expanses without a smile
without a face, without a soul
weary spirals of tubercular sputum
drooping shoulders on fading shadows . . .

Multilingual crossroads knotted to
a confusion of humped roads going nowhere
in a tan-faced coal town—a shame-faced
couple with verdant growths around its loins . . .

Choking smell of antidotes, fighting
the toxic pus freely flowing in deep wounds
festering beneath the bandaged sores of
this laager society going nowhere . . .
Thousands die for this coal town,
state decrees forbid the circulation of rumors,
state diseases are secrets, unremembered
deaths of victims of a dirt-faced nation

with circular roads
going nowhere—

Wankie, 28/1/76

The Redeemer

Here within these confines
bodies resignedly adjust to routine—
the frightening nullifying monotony
behind the barbed-wire reality
in the concrete weird mockery
survival turns man into an explorer
in uncharted worlds, breaks horizons,
to infinite points of imagination rebels
structuring disembodied presences
mocking their emaciated skin covering
this discarded heart in silences.

Elephant skins shield, other bodies
vegetate: rotund bellies, dimpling cheeks
breezes of the great day in reverse
puff bubbles of their egos;
minds equally malleable rest cross-legged
on the symbolic patterns of tribal carpets
weave a web of belching contentment.
The insistent questioning ceases:
contemplate the glory to come.
The sufferer turns self into prophet,
the blinkered visionary reads signs
of futures strewn with glittering crowns.

With a hot fire all seasons, an inert heart,
this prospective prizewinner offers obscene prayers
sees self carrying the torch to the capital.
He declares his resurrection dramatically:
careering along the main street with no brakes
a syphilitic bottom threatens to burst
but stupidity running riot is undaunted.
Welcome: with ululations, black power salutes,
   spreading of carpets and stretched willing virgins
   the pie-faced pumpkin-bellied pensioner
   the struggler prophesying behind eleven bars
   dreaming dreams of pomp and pride:
We subject ourselves to the belly's and bottom's tyranny.

The vegetating potentate, fly-whisk in hand, supporting
props—a hobstick, a harlot, West African gown,
the stage of wavering emotions, wavering
principles and unreliable loves;
the apotheosis
of dreaming-ego-boosting dreamers—
he polishes his rhetoric to match
the flamboyant figure he cuts
this overgrown child of nonsense

Enjoy the drama while you can
take supporting roles; the cast is huge
but do not leave your questioning mind, brother,
to be nibbled in this dance of mice.

1976

My Friends, This Storm

Another day drags its obscenities
the crowded voices disperse reluctantly
declared intentions hang by half-closed doors—
Let night of my days come, let light of my light come
with the wounded silences
our hospital doctorless
shoots prayers, solicitations
that cry come come
to the peace that hides
that has become
treasonable
exiled to the vast prison of the wild.

While our innocence struggles
bloodies itself
disarmed
rages, rages and cries
singing
on chords and tendons of muscled weakness
in the storm
unheeded unatoned—dies
unspoken and unspeaking
   lily-white.

1977

SOLOMON MAHAKA

Solomon Mahaka is a Zimbabwean poet who spent ten years in prison, seven of these in solitary confinement, for political reasons, during the struggle for freedom. His poems have been published in the anthology *And Now the Poets Speak: Poems Inspired by the Struggle for Zimbabwe*, edited by Mudereri Kadhani and Musaemura Zimunya.

In the Zoo

II

Time does not burn you
In our zoo—
It cools you
So that spiders
Can build webs
In your hair,
In peace.

Our zoo is safe
For our abscesses lubricate
This wiry harness
Till it chafes
No more.

There is no hurry here:
The hurry of frantic poets
Struggling to pin down
A recalcitrant image
With a poison-secreting harpoon:
Only the hurry of hurricanes
Shamed by their sins.

We are here:
Far from our forest-seats,
Building castles and computer-mating—
(No longer in sand)—
With the confidence
Of artificial flowers
Standing in vases;
With the innocence of a tear
Rolling down a child's cheek.

As long as cages
Crave fair apes—
And tall trees steal
Lumbermen's hearts of steel—
Our minor zoos
Will love to mushroom
In this great zoo.

If I Leave Here Alive

If I leave here alive
I'll leave nothing behind
They'll never count me
Among the broken men
But I can't say
That I'm normal either.

I've been hungry too long
I've gotten angry too often

I've been lied to and insulted too often
They've pushed me over the line
From where there can be no retreat.

I know they'll not be satisfied
Until they push me out of this existence
Altogether. . . .

I can still smile now
After 10 years of blocking knife-thrusts
And the pick handles of faceless sadists
Of anticipating and reaching for 10 years—
Seven of them in Solitary.

I can still smile sometimes
But by the time this thing is over
I may not be a nice person.

Building Bridges

"Let us build bridges," said he,
"to cross rivers and canyons
and cables to span ocean floors,
Telstar to traverse the vast expanse
of the skies."

We built bridges
And shook hands.

Last night we met,
My friend and I,
two wars old.
Said I to him, "Let us build bridges
to cross rivulets of blood
                    Canals of hate
                    Canyons of prejudice
And furrows of pain."

                    He shook his head
                    And shook his fist.

MUSAEMURA BONUS ZIMUNYA

Musaemura Bonus Zimunya is a Zimbabwean poet who studied at Kent University in England. He first published his poems in *Chirimo*, a Zimbabwean journal, in 1969. Some of his poems have appeared in *STAND*, a British journal, in *Rhodesian Poetry*, and in Kizito Muchemwa's anthology, *Zimbabwean Poetry in English*. He co-edited the anthology *And Now the Poets Speak* with Mudereri Kadhani. The Longman Drumbeat series included his *Thought-Tracks* in 1982. He is Lecturer in English at the University of Zimbabwe.

To a Detainee

That day
ten or twelve years ago
I was full of fear:
police dogs yapping and
salivating like rabid beasts
ringing a hole
whining after the hare—
but there was no hare here.

Termites will eat ironwood,
they can burst through cement,
but they could not consume my fear:
those dogs, those guns,
the twitching nose
under the fierce-looking eyes!
But you were not afraid,
not scared at all.

Human bones
have survived the ravages of time,

and so have yours:
all around you
there used to be shiny steel straight
from African Gate Fences
but the subtle hand of time
has touched you not,
the rust that could not touch human bones
coats the iron with the precision of mold.

I remember well,
we listened,
grandmothers wept,
they sang heavy songs of the earth,
there was ululation and whistling
while frenzied barks
ripped open my spine
and cut through the sounds
like a hack saw on mahogany.

You collected soil,
there was silence,
you refined the grains between your hands
and winnowed them:
"Dogs, trucks and guns belong to them
but the soil, the spirit in the earth
is ours."

Revolution

My brother wrote to tell me
that where once we gathered mushrooms,
things explode and legends and myths
are born,
and ideas emerge: there for the picking.

And in Zimbabwe,
the land produces leaders like
summer mulch,
some titanic, others pygmy,
suddenly bursting out of the dung
at the meagerest tickle of the sunny rain.

I warn you not to be deceived by the top:
vast tumular hordes abound beneath the surface.

Fighter

I was blind and deaf,
I was dumb, and I was palsied.

But now I can see,
I hear, and I mutter, too.
Why, I can even outdance Jikinya.

Fighter,
you made a bow in the sky
And held to the universe a challenge.

Those who walked in a century of darkness
Begin to see the flickering aurora.

The trembling cord long remembers your plucking fingers
And the released shaft finds liberty
In the adder-head of History—
And a bad idea.
Here, a course is terminated.

And though his flesh bears a crater
And a hobnailed cynic leers at his trophy,
See, see his blood streams in the firmament
And behold it whispers dew, dawn and day,
And, more, too, a new thing.

I am the new man
And you are the new woman.
We are heirs of the Rock,
Ne Shirichena, nyakumharapagarwe.
Let him prosper who bends his back
To sow a new idea.

© 1982 Musaemura B. Zimunya. Reprinted from *Thought-Tracks*. By permission
of Longman Group Ltd.
Ne Shirichena, nyakumharapagarwe in Shona refers to the Zimbabwe bird.

The Mountain

We return again to the steep carving
without rope
without wings
groping for the crevices
that our rivalries and greed
make harder and more suspicious to grasp.

Each time we return to the dream
the mountain is steeper
the summit is higher
and the fear is more intense
under the howling cliffs.

We have the terror of waiting at the bottom
knowing there are such head-spinning heights above.
Vaguely, we anticipate the claws of an unknown shadow
if we do not climb to the homely height to freedom
aware that when the dream returns again tonight
the heart has deeper depths to sink under.

It will not be safe to wait for the wrath of midnight
and to deliver the dream into our souls
and compel us to roll the stone up *dzimbahwe*.

We saw each night the mountain turn
and give us a view, each side a portion
of the darkest sky in height
bidding us still to seek for passing shelter
where nature made cave
bidding us still to arrive at the top
where, only where, we could find the rock
to finish the house of Mambo.

Because when daylight comes around
we are prey to the haunting dogma,
the destiny of the stone house brooding over this place.

Dzimbahwe in Shona are houses of stone.
Mambo was the title of the early African rulers of Zimbabwe.

Climbers

We crave for flesh and feet made of earth
and skin made of finest black clay;
we shall praise the potter
with brew of the best grain aferment,
a word of the worthiest prayer
and a cracking stamp of the foot—
dust, indeed, is our eternal shroud.

Bring the song,
you whose voice was the first
to raid into the ancestry of birds,
you whose horn was a throat in the kingdom of birds,
and let your tongue tremble,
you whose ululation seized the wind
and trapped it within the mouth of mankind—
your song is a goddess at the dawn of the heart.

Bring the drum,
you who prolonged the bellow of the ox
beyond the axe of the butcher
with the touch of the fired palm
and made the dry days echo again
into the post-winter haze of the tropic—
your dance is a god waiting in the heart.

Give us feet that can climb the giddiest mountain
and hands that will clasp the tenderest tufts
and heads that will level the dizziest heights
so that we can bring the rock down to Zimbabwe.
For there is the shell of our soul.

Comforts of one warm winter
did not stop the mamba
from seeking a burrow for a cold season.

A fat summer drove the ant into harder industry
more aware of the coming winter.

Even the crow ensured his plenty,
burying cakes of pilfered soap
although his amnesia ensured its loss,
for there was no risk to be taken.

Give us the heart that transcends greed,
give us the heads that rise beyond our burrows
and be ours the eyes that shoot unto the stars
on the darkest, cloudiest night.

One hand to another,
one rock to another,
one rock over the other,
one wall inside another,
outside another until
the city towers above the trees
and we all look up at the dream
taller than potbellies, higher than collars,
whisks, uniforms, and accents,
higher still than skyscrapers

To remind us, down-trodden and ignorant,
remind us, you who have the wisdom,
to climb even higher than Mambo
and put an enduring roof upon this House.

ABOUT THE EDITOR

Frank Chipasula, a Malawian poet now in exile, is
currently a teaching assistant in the English department
at Brown University, where he is also a Ph.D. candidate in
English literature. He attended the University of
Malawi, received a B.A. from the University of Zambia
in 1976, M.A.s from Brown in 1980 and from Yale
University in 1982. He was English editor of NECZAM
(National Publishers) in Lusaka, Zambia, from 1976 to
1978, and received the Soche Annual Peace Prize,
endowed by Paul Theroux. He is the author of
Visions and Reflections: A Collection of Poems and
O Earth, Wait for Me, and editor of *A Decade in Poetry*,
an anthology of Zambian poetry. He lives in Providence,
Rhode Island.

ABOUT THE BOOK

This book was typeset by Heritage Printers, Inc., of
Charlotte, North Carolina, in Linotype Granjon with
Monotype Garamond display, and was printed at
Heritage by letterpress on 60-pound Olde Style paper
manufactured by the S. D. Warren Company of Boston.
It was bound by Kingsport Press of Kingsport, Tennessee.
The design is by Joyce Kachergis Book Design and
Production of Bynum, North Carolina.

Wesleyan University Press, 1985